CHARLES CHAPLIN

An Appreciation

Charles Silver

The Museum of Modern Art, New York

FOR BO SMITH AND MARY LEA BANDY

Published in conjunction with the exhibition "Chaplin: A Centennial Celebration"
at The Museum of Modern Art, New York, January 1–June 30, 1989

This project has been made possible with generous support from
Celeste G. Bartos, Pinewood Foundation, and Kimiko and John Powers.

The Museum's film program is made possible in part through the support of
The Roy and Niuta Titus Fund, the National Endowment for the Arts, Washington, D.C.,
and with public funds from the New York State Council on the Arts.

Edited by James Leggio
Designed by Barbara Balch Design, New York
Production by Daniel Frank
Set in type by Graphic Technology, Inc., New York
Printed by Allied Printing Services, Inc., Manchester, Connecticut
Bound by Mueller Trade Bindery, Middletown, Connecticut

All photographs from the Film Stills Archive,
The Museum of Modern Art, New York

Distributed outside the United States and Canada
by Thames and Hudson Ltd., London

The Museum of Modern Art
11 West 53 Street
New York, New York 10019

Printed in the United States of America

First page: Jackie Coogan and Chaplin in *The Kid*, 1921
Frontispiece: Chaplin in *The Gold Rush*, 1925
Back cover: Chester Conklin and Chaplin in *Modern Times*, 1936

CONTENTS

ACKNOWLEDGMENTS

April 16, 1989, marks the centennial of the birth of Charlie Chaplin, later Charles Chaplin, and, after March 4, 1975, Sir Charles Chaplin. This publication is part of The Museum of Modern Art's celebration of that historic occasion, which will also include an exhibition of posters and film stills and a retrospective of Chaplin's feature-length motion pictures.

For their patience and goodwill during the preparation of this book, I am especially indebted to Ron Magliozzi and Nancy Barnes, my colleagues in the Film Study Center of The Museum of Modern Art. My editor, James Leggio, of the Museum's Department of Publications, Mary Corliss of the Museum's Film Stills Archive, and Rachel Gallagher, who prepared the filmography, have also been very helpful. I would like to thank Moses Rothman for his support of our Chaplin celebration and Jeff Saxon of Universal Pictures for enabling me to see *A Countess from Hong Kong*. Thanks, too, to the Film Society of Lincoln Center for permitting us to reprint my article "The Second Coming" from *Film Comment*. On a personal note of gratitude, as head of the Film Study Center, I would like to express my indebtedness to Celeste Bartos for her very generous support of our research facilities and program, and in particular for her support of this publication.

The literature on Chaplin is voluminous. David Robinson's *Chaplin: His Life and Art* (New York: McGraw-Hill, 1985) has become the definitive biography, superseding those by Theodore Huff and John McCabe, among others. I recommend reading Robinson's book in tandem with Chaplin's own *My Autobiography* (New York: Simon & Schuster, 1964). Both James Agee and Andrew Sarris are particularly insightful on the subject in their collected reviews.

Chaplin in *The Circus*

INTRODUCTION

Seventy-five years ago, in February 1914—six months before the guns of August signaled the beginning of the end—a messiah for the modern age appeared. He was a figure of shabby elegance and decidedly dubious dignity, a denizen of the slums. In short, he was a bum, or as his creator preferred, a tramp. Scrambling for survival against uneven odds and frequently giving the representatives of authority a forceful kick in the butt, the tramp attracted the allegiance of that mass of humanity for which the twentieth century offered a threatening present and a potentially dire future. His adherents' admiration of the butt-kicking facility of this "gentleman of nerve" was matched by their intuitive understanding that Charlie Chaplin gave to the movies an inimitable and barely definable gift. In a fairly short time, slumming intellectuals began to test the limits of language trying to explain the messianic power of this "little fellow." From our contemporary perspective it is obvious that Chaplin brought a range and depth of acting, a subtlety of performance, that has never been approached by the multitude whose faces and movements have been flashed across cinema screens. No particular level of sophistication or even literacy was necessary, however, to see that he was special: you only had to *see.*

The phenomenon of Chaplin's immense worldwide popularity was more than anything the result of the happiest of cultural accidents. For all but his last five films, Chaplin required no language, or rather his language was universal and elemental. Although he was clearly a white male dealing with the hazards of a Western society, his feelings and values were not restricted by geography or milieu. Everyone understood loneliness, everyone looked for love, and everyone longed to kick someone in the butt. Chaplin elevated the most basic human needs and vulnerabilities to the highest levels of art. In the process, he touched more people, more deeply, than any artist in human history, and he is touching us still. This book is offered as a tribute and appreciation to commemorate the centenary of his birth.

Chaplin was understandably prone to refer to the "feebleness" of words, and I would be the first to acknowledge that nothing written can substitute for the experience of the films themselves. I can only hope to encourage you to see them, and perhaps add a little to your pleasure. See the films and see if you agree that Charlie Chaplin—ultimately Sir Charles—will do nicely still, until another messiah comes along.

THREE EARLY FEATURES:
THE KID, 1921   THE PILGRIM, 1923
A WOMAN OF PARIS, 1923

There is much that is rich and rewarding in the seventy shorts Chaplin made in his early years and much that tantalizingly hints at his future, even in the most primitive works of the Keystone period. As was true with D. W. Griffith's films at the Biograph Studio, Chaplin was learning his craft and polishing his skills. And as Griffith did, Chaplin often borrowed the ideas of his youth for further development and refinement in his later, more ambitious works. The focus of this book is on these feature films, the products of his maturity from 1921 to 1967.

It was a natural thing for Chaplin to want to move beyond the constraints of two-reel (approximately thirty minutes) comedies, and he had already attempted to do so in *A Dog's Life* (1918), *Shoulder Arms* (1918), and *Sunnyside* (1919). *The Kid* (1921), however, represented something far more challenging than a move to feature-length. Chaplin was now grasping, probably half-consciously, for an immortality that he felt might elude him in a perpetual stream of seemingly ephemeral two-reelers. The death of his first-born son had brought the first note of genuine tragedy to his adult life, and his business struggles with First National Studio hinted forebodingly at the possibility that he might not be able to continue to make pictures

forever. *The Kid* was intended to leave an indelible mark, and it did.

The opening title announces, "A picture with a smile—and perhaps a tear." In essence, this was to become a manifesto for the balance of Chaplin's career. Being adored as the world's funniest man was no longer to be enough. With *The Kid*, a streak of poignancy and melancholy, only hinted at before, was to infuse his work. To his detractors, who eventually grew to be legion in at least some circles of the intelligentsia, his "sentimentality," "manipulation," and "solipsism" became a fatal flaw. Chaplin's supporters argued that the depth of feeling in his films and the expertness of his execution were more than ample compensation for any excesses. The cinema, after all, surpassed all previous artificial means of evoking human emotion, and Chaplin (like Griffith before him and John Ford after) was using the powerfully expressive tool at his command to dredge from within himself something primal and authentic. As I wrote at the occasion of his death: "To criticize Chaplin as too sentimental is to deny our own potential for vulnerability and feeling. To view him as self-indulgent for exposing his own feelings on film is to constrict the cinema to the dimensions of other media, or worse yet, to see movies as mere technical or academic exercises.

Jackie Coogan and Chaplin

Simply put, one misses the point."

The Kid is ultimately a love story between the Tramp and a five-year-old boy, Jackie Coogan. It is set in the dingy memory-world of Chaplin's childhood (vividly chronicled in both his autobiography and in David Robinson's excellent biography). Throughout his career, Chaplin evoked images of the Dickensian poverty from which he had emerged, scenes of tiny, fallen-down flats, flea-infested flophouses, and sinister streets inhabited by thugs and, even more threatening to the Tramp, the forces of law and reform.

In this context, it is easy to think of the waifish Coogan as a reincarnation of young Charlie, receiving from the Tramp the paternal love largely denied to Chaplin by his father's dalliance and alcoholism. Edna Purviance is the fallen woman ("whose sin was motherhood") who abandons Coogan when he is an infant, later reconsiders, and then spends years searching for the child. Chaplin's own mother drifted in and out of madness and was never quite able to provide a lasting home for Charlie and his older half-brother, Sydney. The ending of *The Kid*, with the reunion of mother, son, and surrogate father in apparent domestic bliss and material comfort, seems a bit too fast and facile, but one senses a pressing need for Chaplin to reflect on what might have been.

In *The Kid*, the Tramp has already become relatively bourgeois by the standards of many ear-

lier Chaplin films. He has a home, be it ever so humble, an occupation (repairing windows broken, felicitously, by Coogan a few minutes before), and a reluctant willingness to undertake the commitment of fatherhood. (Before he takes the baby home, Charlie tries returning him to the garbage heap in which he was found, makes him a second passenger in a briefly unattended pram, and even toys with dumping him in a sewer.) Finally acquiescing, the Tramp approaches his parental responsibilities somewhat like an artist for whom the child is a canvas fit for a self-portrait. In contemporary parlance, the Tramp's parenting produces a loving and lovable clone.

Elemental sustenance is at the source of much of the conflict in Chaplin's films, and food is typically one of the major comedy motifs of *The Kid*. Charlie serves up large portions of an exceptionally gloppy stew from a bucket, and the boy makes a huge pile of pancakes to be scrupulously divided between them. Their love for each other is measured out in precise quantities of nourishment, with actors Charlie and Jackie's hilarious performances never detracting from director Chaplin's insistence on the nasty naturalism of penury.

One of the great virtues of *The Kid*, something true of all Chaplin's best work, is that a heavy aura of reality hovers (with an exception to be noted later) over the fantasy and mayhem. His world is one of great physicality, often bordering on the vulgar. He forces us to consider Jackie's toilet training, inspects the boy's head for lice, and belches after a heavy dose of pancakes. In his last film, *A Countess from Hong Kong*, the final memory we have of Chaplin's acting career is his being about to vomit from seasickness. By emphasizing the essential frailty of human beings, including himself, Chaplin makes it all the more remarkable that such creatures can rise to heights of tenderness, sacrifice, and grace. The "vulgarity" in mature Chaplin is never gratuitous, merely his reminder of who we are, and that he is one of us.

There is a tiny moment in *The Kid* which illuminates his obsession with the nitty-gritty. Flophouse manager Henry Bergman is reading a Yiddish newspaper. There is a long close-up of Edna's advertisement offering a reward for the boy, and for a split second a fly crawls up the page. Surely, Chaplin's masterly skills did not extend to directing this insect, and it was clearly unplanned. But being the meticulous editor he was, he must have noticed the fly and decided to use that particular take. The artist in him told him it was right that there should be a fly in a flophouse.

The Kid is in many ways a product of its time. It uses such visual devices as the iris effect common to the melodramas of the period and reflecting the pervasive influence of D. W. Griffith. Like Griffith, Chaplin indulges in now-dated symbolism (some of which he cut from the re-release version of 1971), much of it religious in nature, surprising in light of the attacks later in his life from Christian zealots. There are certainly echoes of Griffith's *Intolerance* (1916) in the satirization of the do-gooders who try to take Jackie away to the orphan asylum. One also wonders whether Chaplin saw King Vidor's *The Jackknife Man*, a lovely film released five months

before *The Kid* by the same studio, First National. There are a number of suggestive similarities between the two movies.

Toward the end of *The Kid*, after Jackie disappears from the flophouse, Chaplin presents us with a bizarre and perhaps unfathomable dream sequence. In the dream, the Tramp seems to go to heaven, where everyone flies about on angel wings. At first glance, this appears to be offered as an alternative to earthly suffering, but the idyll ends when devils intrude, temptation and lust become rampant, and Charlie is shot down and awakens in the clutches of human law, more hopeless than ever. It all ends happily, of course, but this sequence remains, for me at least, an inexplicable flaw in the film. Whatever its intent, Chaplin had broken his cardinal rule of not drifting too far from a comprehensible reality. The law summons him to Edna's mansion, where he is reunited with Jackie. Because of the confusion induced by the dream sequence, and since the attraction between Charlie and Edna had never been developed, the viewer is left with some anxiety as to what their future together might bring.

The emotional high point, the most satisfying moment in *The Kid*, had occurred two reels before, after the boy is heroically and hysterically rescued from the asylum van. In a prolonged close-up, boy and man tearfully kiss each other on the lips, one of the cinema's most privileged moments of profound sincerity and pure innocence.

The Pilgrim (1923) is a charming little film (less than four reels) made to fulfill Chaplin's contract with First National. It differs from his short films in the richness of its satirical characterizations and in a certain idiosyncratic and introspective quality he brought to the project.

According to the memoirs of the sculptor Clare

Sheridan, Chaplin had in 1922 propounded a theory of the similarity of mind between the artist and the criminal, both sharing "a deep sense of unlawfulness." (This was to be a major implication of *Monsieur Verdoux,* a quarter-century later.) As the Pilgrim, an escaped convict masquerading as a minister, but still the ineffable Tramp, Chaplin demonstrates the blending of larcenous and artistic skills. The Pilgrim, with his ingenious pantomime of David and Goliath, converts his church first into a courtroom, then a saloon, and ultimately a theater. The graying actor had by now developed his timing, gestures, and facial expressions to an unprecedented level of performance. *The Pilgrim* provided him with the opportunity for showing off his theatrical magic

and commenting frankly on his ability to deceive an audience with the sleight-of-mind that was his unique gift. Surely, Chaplin did not believe that the hicks of Devil's Gulch were representative of his own following, but it must have pleased him immensely to picture himself as a phony clergyman so easily gulling the ignorant. Here, perhaps, we are seeing the first small cracks in the relationship between Chaplin and his public, later to become a chasm.

Evoking so many of the films he made in the preceding decade, *The Pilgrim* is a kind of summing-up or valediction, before Chaplin embarks on the "serious" *A Woman of Paris.* There is something almost self-deprecating in an extraordinary tracking shot (camera movement was rare in his work) in which a naughty boy knowingly looks at the camera and then deliberately throws a banana peel in the path of the Pilgrim and the fat deacon, Mack Swain. Of course, both obligingly slip and fall, and it is funny, even more so for our anticipation. However, by having the boy acknowledge the camera and, hence, our presence, Chaplin seems to be telling us that pratfalls are now too easy for him—his facility with such nonsense has become too great—and he must move on to bigger things.

The irony of such self-condescension is that Chaplin could hardly be funnier than he is in *The Pilgrim*. Whether shaking an old man's beard, kicking drawers shut while riding piggyback on the villain, or engaging in a duel of wits with a vicious toddler, Chaplin provides a compendium of classic, perfectly executed slapstick treasures.

Sadly, an even greater irony occurs at the film's conclusion, one not to be understood until a generation later. The Pilgrim straddles the border between Mexico and the United States, caught precariously between bullet-throwing bandits and a sheriff who has expelled him from Texas. Chaplin could not conceivably have anticipated his future problems with American law and his ultimate exclusion from his adopted homeland. But in retrospect, the final image of *The Pilgrim* becomes haunting and ominous, almost prescient.

A *Woman of Paris* (1923) is subtitled *A Drama of Fate*. Although it has occasional moments of humor, Chaplin adhered closely to his intention of showing, as David Robinson has put it, "the inner workings of the mind and heart through external signs . . . the range, subtlety and sophistication of the sentiments and motives that could be revealed in pictures." Hence, *A Woman of Paris* became a film of delicate nuance: no room

for banana peels or the Tramp, here.

In order to establish a context for his seriousness of purpose, the director seemed to borrow in the early sequences from the masterworks of German and Swedish Expressionism. Indeed, he may have seen such films as Victor Sjöström's *The Phantom Chariot* (1921), but it is worth noting that Chaplin's own 1918 short *The Bond* has its share of experimental effects of lighting and decor.

On its own terms, *A Woman of Paris* was and remains an enormous success. As Lillian Gish's sole comedic performance in *His Double Life* (1933) attests to the fact that this great tragedian could have succeeded on the road not taken, so Chaplin proved that he had talent and resources undisclosed by his comedies. Much has been written of the film's great influence on Ernst Lubitsch, his string of disciples, and a host of imitators. In fact, the very novelty of Chaplin's direction at the time tends to limit the impact that *A Woman of Paris* can have now, on contemporary audiences. Too much of what was almost shockingly new in 1923 has become familiar by its overuse in other films, and we long for Charlie's presence on-screen to remind us that this is, indeed, a Chaplin work. The language of gestures signifying repressed emotions was a fresh invention in 1923, and it is to Chaplin's credit that it was used not just by Lubitsch, but by other titans from Sternberg to Stroheim, Renoir to Ford. Unfortunately, removed as we are by sixty-five years of film history, it is difficult now to discern in the limited though undeniable pleasures of *A Woman of Paris* the work of genius it was considered in its time.

Even the dedicated film historian must make an effort to reimagine how vital the works of the silent screen looked in their original context. And, of course, there are further barriers to full appreciation. There are gaps of lost films, while those that survive are often tattered and scratchy. And there

Edna Purviance and Adolphe Menjou

are the obvious problems of antiquated costumes and manners unfamiliar to what we think of as our more sophisticated, modern minds.

We have become accustomed to classifying the truly great silent movies into two categories: those with devastating performances by the likes of Lillian Gish, Falconetti, or Chaplin himself, and those visually compelling works like Griffith's *Intolerance*, Eisenstein's *Potemkin*, or Murnau's *Sunrise* which overwhelm us with their grandeur and style. Chaplin's direction of *A Woman of Paris* seems by comparison too constrained; his canvas is too small, and his own absence from the screen creates an unavoidable vacuum.

This is his last film with Edna Purviance, his leading lady since 1915, and it had been his hope to finally make her a star in her own right. Purviance, however, already becoming a bit plump and

Edna Purviance, Carl Miller, and Adolphe Menjou

matronly at twenty-nine, lacks the requisite aura and is never much more than serviceable. She had been an excellent comic foil from *A Night Out* to *The Pilgrim* (somewhat akin to Diane Keaton's function in several Woody Allen movies), but the demands of this "victim of fate" role seem just beyond her range.

Adolphe Menjou, of course, was to parlay his suave man-of-the-world into a distinguished career, most notably in Josef von Sternberg's *Morocco* (1930). His debonair dignity is perfect for Chaplin's purposes, enlivening the melodramatic plot conventions with quicksilver grace and charm. With the possible exceptions of Jackie Coogan in *The Kid* and Claire Bloom in *Limelight,* Menjou gives the best performance in any Chaplin film, except for Charlie's own.

Here, again, we return to the fundamental problem and the reason *A Woman of Paris* failed commer-

cially. Audiences were not prepared to accept a Chaplin film without Charlie, even one that was critically acclaimed. Other than his brief, disguised walk-on as a railway porter, a Chaplinesque cameo by a studio secretary playing a masseuse, and an ending in which Purviance and Menjou pass each other on a dusty country road (traveling toward their respective destinies, by now a familiar Chaplin metaphor), there was no particular reason to associate *A Woman of Paris* with the comic genius who created *The Kid* and *The Pilgrim.* It was just another melodrama, albeit unusually skillful, with too much coincidence and convention. The subtleties sought and generally achieved by the director were lost on the ticket-buying public. The bitterness of this disappointment led him to suppress the film for half a century. The proud creator of *A Woman of Paris* had himself become a "victim of fate."

THE GOLD RUSH
1925

One of the key intertitles in *A Woman of Paris* informs us that "the secret of happiness is in service to others." With his next film, Chaplin returned to the service he was uniquely capable of rendering—making us laugh. *The Gold Rush* (1925), *The Circus* (1928), *City Lights* (1931), and *Modern Times* (1936) were to be an unbroken string of comic masterpieces, establishing the director's strong claim to being the preeminent artist of the silent cinema. (In fairness, one must note that Chaplin's financial resources and independence enabled him to extend the silent era for many years beyond what was permitted to such rivals as Griffith, Murnau, and Buster Keaton.)

At various times, Chaplin spoke of *The Gold Rush* as his most accomplished work, partly, I would think, because its enormous popular success restored his confidence after the commercial disappointment of *A Woman of Paris*. Certainly for the first time, he wove his comedic and dramatic talents into a seamless tapestry. It may be more of a personal quibble than anything else, but I have always been less moved by *The Gold Rush* than by the three films that followed it. Perhaps this reflects the dislocation one feels at finding the Tramp in Alaska, removed from his familiar urban surroundings. There is a sense one has that the "little fellow" has wandered into someone else's movie, another cineaste's world. It's somewhat akin to the unease of seeing John Wayne in a non-Western, even the great John Ford films like *They Were Expendable* or *The Quiet Man*.

There is also the problem of a too-resolute ending to *The Gold Rush*. It is somehow easier to accept the ambiguous conclusions of *The Kid* or *City Lights* or the tragic disappointment of *The Circus*. *Modern Times* ends with Charlie and Paulette Goddard happily setting off together down the road, but this at least leaves open the possibility of further adventure and struggle. Personally, I can't quite come to grips with the concept of the Tramp becoming a married millionaire. One can only presume that Chaplin had resolved finally to retire the Tramp, resenting his dependence on the character and wishing him well and good riddance. Of course, this was not to be the case. In *The Circus*, *City Lights*, and *Modern Times*, Chaplin would turn inward, and the Tramp was to be the soulful embodiment of his efforts to make comic sense of a tortured personal life and a world in disarray. *The Gold Rush* seems less profoundly mature than its successors, reflecting as it does the final glimmers of Chaplin's youth.

Chaplin spent a great deal of money and time with his location shooting in an effort to give an air

of authenticity to *The Gold Rush.* If his audience didn't want the psychological realism of *A Woman of Paris,* he would at least provide them with photographic naturalism. (Robert Flaherty's *Nanook of the North* had been a popular success only three years before, establishing the public's interest in documentaries.) Here, he was making his closest approach to the work of the great Buster Keaton, who used realistic natural settings to anchor his brilliant physical comedy and manic visual gags.

A recurring plot device of *The Gold Rush* is that of the Tramp and other characters being lost in the white Alaskan wilderness. Of course, metaphorically, Charlie is always lost, even when he is in the various hovels that he considers home. He never fits

in with the established order; he is a fugitive from everyone else's reality. His efforts to enter the mainstream of life are as futile as his hilarious attempts early in the film to leave the cabin, repeatedly being blown backward by the force of the gusting wind each time he opens the door.

Chaplin has two major relationships in the film, with Mack Swain and Georgia Hale. The one with Swain is by far the more sincere and reciprocally loving. The huge actor with bulging eyes had worked with him at Keystone in 1914 and later appeared in *The Idle Class, Pay Day,* and, of course, *The Pilgrim.* The camaraderie of the tiny Chaplin and the monstrous Swain anticipated the teamwork of Stan Laurel and Oliver Hardy by two years. Like

Chaplin and Mack Swain

Stan and Ollie's, Charlie and Mack's relationship has overtones and undercurrents of an innocent homosexuality. On their first meeting, Chaplin gingerly pets Swain as one might a gigantic dog whose intentions have not yet become apparent. Later, he flirts with him to win his support against the villainous Black Larsen, making highly seductive eye movements. Swain is childlike, and his relationship with Charlie assumes some of the characteristics of Jackie Coogan's in *The Kid*: when they are starving, Charlie tries to provide for him by cooking a shoe. In the process of preparing and eating this "feast," Chaplin's daintiness and gentility border on effeminacy. When the shoe fails to provide adequate nourishment and Swain becomes delirious, he hallucinates that Charlie is a giant chicken. In this state of mind, Mack loves Charlie so much he wants literally to eat him up. Later in the

Georgia Hale and Chaplin

film, the amnesiac Swain violently pulls Chaplin away from Georgia, requiring his help in rediscovering his lost mountain of gold.

None of this is meant to imply any conscious attempt on Chaplin's part to suggest a sexual attraction. Unconsciously, however, there is a strong theme of men being able to trust other men in his films, juxtaposed with the recurrent unreliability of the women he pursues. In *City Lights,* for example,

he falls asleep in the same bed with playboy-millionaire Harry Myers, who awakens with surprise and an expression equivalent to the standard disclaimer, "Boy, was I drunk last night!" Chaplin had appeared in convincing drag in several early films, and his attempts at anything approaching "macho" were always in the context of self-mockery. He frequently indicated that his closest relationship was with Douglas Fairbanks, until the latter's death

in 1939. Given the disastrous results of his real-life experiences with women to that date and the acknowledged feminine side of his nature, it is hardly surprising that sexual ambiguity, and even a certain androgyny, receive occasional expression in his work.

In spite of its one-sidedness, Chaplin's interaction with Georgia Hale in *The Gold Rush* is his first major attempt at portraying a genuinely romantic relationship in his comedies. Previously, Edna Purviance (and her predecessors, notably Mabel Normand) had been either a comic foil or a peripheral aspect of the plot. Even in *The Kid*, Edna's feelings were directed almost exclusively toward Jackie Coogan, not the Tramp. Although Georgia is insincere and cruel, there is a complexity and finally a redeeming quality to her character.

Georgia Hale, discovered in Josef von Sternberg's low-budget first feature, *The Salvation Hunters* (1925), and plucked from obscurity, replaced Chaplin's pregnant wife, Lita Grey. She does not appear in the opening third of the film, and Chaplin reintroduces her several times with intertitles, as though he were afraid that she was too forgettable. Audiences seemed to confirm that apprehension, since her career survived only three years. Her performance, like her role as a pretty but mindless girl, is primarily functional, giving Chaplin comic opportunities and a fantasy love-object. (Juicier female roles would have to await the appearance of larger talents like Paulette Goddard, Martha Raye, Claire Bloom, and Sophia Loren.) For the most part, Hale is a passive observer of such delightful slapstick scenes as Charlie's entanglement with a dog, as he dances with her, and his feather-covered rapture when she unexpectedly returns to his cabin after they had made a date for New Year's Eve.

It is no secret that Chaplin tended to be attracted to younger women lacking his intensity and intelligence, and in his early efforts to portray romantic love on the screen, it was to be expected that the fantasy women he created would border on being ciphers. Virginia Cherrill in *City Lights* is the extreme case because she is blind and, one senses, virtually nonexistent when out of Chaplin's sight. It is a tribute to Paulette Goddard's effect on him (off and on-screen) that she was able to break this mold in *Modern Times* and become a worthy soulmate.

But in *The Gold Rush,* Chaplin's comic inspiration reaches its peak in scenes with Mack Swain—eating the shoe, the chicken delusion, and the climactic moment where their cabin teeters on the brink of the precipice. Georgia, on the other hand, remains incidental, almost a prop, in the comic set pieces in which she appears. Indeed, the American silent cinema is largely devoid of major young comediennes, with the notable exceptions of Mabel Normand and, toward the end of the era, Marion Davies and Colleen Moore. In a sense, women were still standing on a Victorian pedestal, too dignified and sacrosanct for the rough-and-tumble of physical fun.

Georgia is present as a spectator in Charlie's dream, in which he performs the poetic dance of the rolls. Here, with only his face and hands, Chaplin shows the cinema's capacity for transforming the simplest moments into shining epiphanies. His sublime grace in this sequence—like Garbo standing expressionless and absolutely still in the last shot of Mamoulian's *Queen Christina* or John Wayne framed in the closing door at the end of Ford's *The Searchers*—demonstrates beyond argument that the quintessence of film art has very little to do with vast technical resources or visual razzle-dazzle. Film, albeit the most mechanical of the arts, ultimately belongs more to human beings, to faces, than to machines.

Paradoxically, the movie which gives us the quixotic and gentle dance of the rolls is also Chaplin's most violent (at least before *The Great Dictator* and *Monsieur Verdoux* appeared in the era of Hitler and Hiroshima). Several characters are actually killed during *The Gold Rush,* and Charlie must contend with guns, knives, axes, fire, precipices, bears, and bullies, to say nothing of starvation. The Tramp had always had to worry about the police, but they were usually hilariously inept and threatened, at worst, a night in a sheltering jail cell. The slapstick brutality of his early work was stylized and caused no lasting harm. But now, being actually beaten, bitten, shot, stabbed, or even eaten provided a new dimension of real terror in a comedy. Even the Great War in *Shoulder Arms* was less menacing. Perhaps this sense of actual danger was a carryover from the naturalistic impulse that motivated *A Woman of Paris,* or possibly it reflected the gloom of Chaplin's personal life at the time. In any case, it clearly anticipated

the revelations of the darker and more serious side of his personality which would dominate his work two decades later.

Another significant change had occurred since *The Kid.* Many of the supporting characters in early slapstick comedies, including Chaplin's, had been grossly stylized, to the point of being virtual cardboard cutouts or cartoons. These grotesquely made-up actors with broad acting styles (if acting is the word for their excess in manner and gesture) had little in common with anybody who actually walked the earth. With *The Gold Rush*, Chaplin began to take greater care to make these peripheral people credible, and there are memorable moments provided by them which lend the film a rounded quality previously lacking in his work. This is particularly true in the several scenes shot in the Monte Carlo dance hall, where grizzled prospectors are given their instant or two of immortality, vignettes lingering on screen long enough to stick in our memory. When Charlie, disappointed by Georgia's failure to appear for his meticulously prepared New Year's party, hears "Auld Lang Syne" drifting across the snow from the Monte Carlo, we see him in tearful close-up, excluded once again from society and the love of his fellow creatures. The genuine poignancy of the event is accentuated, however, when Chaplin cuts back to the dance hall for close-ups of various patrons either pensive or crying, each with their own private memories and pain. This belies the charge of Chaplin's so-called solipsistic self-pity, and it speaks (ever so silently) to the universality of loneliness and Chaplin's recognition of our common human frailty.

The Tramp is, of course, the perennial and permanent outsider, the stranger in the strangest of lands, looking in the window at the brightly lit party, himself a shadowy silhouette in the darkness. When he is invited to take part, it is the result of accident or mistaken identity, or he is being used as a tool by another person. He is a character on the edge of the film strip clinging gamely to the sprocket holes, unable to enter the frame where life is happening, where people are having fun, where others are taking and giving love. And this, in spite of the ironic fact that it is, after all, *his* film.

As in *A Woman of Paris*, Chaplin makes much of "Fate" taking charge of human affairs. In *The Gold Rush* natural forces, storms and avalanches, control destinies, separate people and reunite them, and sometimes destroy them. No matter how harrowing his adventures, Charlie always finds the resources to recover and survive. Through it all, when his pants are falling down, his face is covered with snow, his hair is full of feathers, and his foot is on fire, he strives to maintain a semblance of dignity. While mistaken for a chicken or burying a gun in the snow with hindquarter kicks like a dog, he remains only human, suffused with those qualities and capacities we all share, but which Chaplin had in such abundance and diversity. Fate finally made the Tramp a millionaire (as it had Charles Spencer Chaplin), but only for one reel. After the successful rush for gold, the artist found that what truly glittered still eluded him.

THE CIRCUS
1928

The Tramp, who had achieved wealth and celebrity at the end of *The Gold Rush,* reappears in *The Circus* "hungry and broke." If one accepts that Chaplin's films are, at least on one level, autobiographical meditations with the Tramp as his surrogate, how does one account for this discrepancy? Perhaps the explanation lies in his lifelong insecurity, his inescapable memory of poverty and homelessness. Indeed, when his public and the U.S. government turned on him in the years following World War II, Chaplin's paranoia became a self-fulfilling prophecy—for although he never lost his wealth, he did lose his adopted homeland and the adoration of the multitude. All along, Chaplin might have felt the Tramp was most protected when he had nothing left to lose.

Seen from the distance of six decades, *The Circus* is clearly one of Chaplin's most self-reflective films, both personally and professionally. Only *Limelight,* with its extended ruminations on romantic love and the craft of comedy, rivals it, and *The Circus* has the virtue of being sublimely succinct in its silence. The plots of the two films are parallel—giving up the girl to a more virile, younger man while trying to maintain one's grasp on an elusive comic muse.

The concept of personal artistry in the cinema has always had to contend with the substantive myth that it is a collaborative medium, the coming together of the talents of directors, producers, writers, technicians, craftsmen, and, of course, actors. Chaplin had the special advantage (shared with Buster Keaton, Orson Welles, and, more recently, Woody Allen) of starring in his own work. That the director/writer/producer Chaplin was fortunate enough to have the screen's premier actor at his disposal, and that all these personae understood precisely what the others were trying to achieve, made them (him) uniquely adept at transforming abstract inspiration into tangible celluloid. In no other instance, it must be assumed, did the image on the screen so closely approximate the original conception in the director's mind.

Through his working methods (rehearsing and experimenting on film ad infinitum, throwing away all that did not meet his standard), Chaplin had the additional advantage of delving into the depths of his mind and heart for exactly what it was he wanted to express. In this, he comes closest of anyone with a camera to approaching the solitary act of scratching with a pen on a blank page. What he was doing, in essence, was using the whole mechanical apparatus of his own movie studio to say, in the manner of a diarist: "This is my life, these are my feelings, this is me." Therefore, I would

Merna Kennedy and Chaplin

argue that it is futile to try to separate Chaplin the actor from Chaplin the director/writer/producer, as some have attempted to do. The former's face and body were the vessels through which the latter sought expression, but they are all one person with a singular capacity to communicate feelings and offer the audience the most intimate of gifts—himself.

Lest this all sound a bit too serious, it should be pointed out that *The Circus* is one of the purest and funniest comedies ever made. It moves fast, and it is encumbered by very little plot or (until the end) pathos. The climactic sequence (Chaplin's original inspiration for the film), in which Charlie is beset by a horde of escaped monkeys while walking a tight-rope, is about as riotous as any sequence in any movie. Several primal fears are confronted simul-

taneously as Charlie struggles to maintain his balance at a great height, while his pants are falling down, and furry beasts are biting his nose and sticking their tails in his mouth.

Alfred Hitchcock, who shared Chaplin's London roots and creative exile in Hollywood, understood that our worst nightmares could be a source of considerable humor, and that laughter might be our only defense against the terrors which lurked in our (or, more fiendishly, in his) imagination. As with the teetering cabin at the end of *The Gold Rush*, Chaplin makes us laugh hysterically at the extremes of human desperation and fear, and, by extension, at our own endless scramble for survival.

The Tramp aspires to the aerial grace of the tightrope-walker in the hope of winning over the lovely Merna Kennedy by elevating himself, liter-

ally, to a higher plane of dignity. Dignity is a major issue in *The Circus*.

In his clown class, Charlie rebuffs efforts in a barbershop skit to provide him with a faceful of shaving cream, rebuking his teacher for this symbolic retreat to his Mack Sennett days. When he accidentally throws a pie in another actor's face, he denies involvement, attributing the mess to a passing bird. The same actor is humiliated when

Charlie forces him to bend over so that he can strike a match on his behind. *The Circus* is, in fact, overloaded with anal jokes, a festival of butt-kicking. The derriere is, of course, man's foremost reminder that his pretensions to civilization and to superiority over the animals hide a simpler truth. Chaplin's point is that beneath our thin costume and the dignified role-playing it engenders lies an enduring potential for baseness.

We are in many ways the weakest and most vulnerable of species, and *The Circus* contains repeated insinuations of the inferiority of humans to their animal captives. Human dignity (mostly Charlie's) is subjected to a variety of assaults at the hands, or rather the hooves and paws, of an ornery mule, a rebellious horse, a sleepy lion, a yappy dog, a wiggly worm, assorted ducks, pigs, and rabbits, and, of course, the monkeys. Despite assertions of nobility and control, man is at the mercy of the world's menagerie, a view which receives its most profoundly anal expression three years later in *City Lights,* in a statement made by a passing pachyderm.

In *The Circus,* only Merna Kennedy, as the current embodiment of Chaplin's idealized femininity, is able to maintain dominance over the animals, riding her horse around the ring as though she were standing on a moving pedestal. By the time the film was in production, it had become evident that

Chaplin's second marriage (to Lita Grey) was an even greater disaster than his first (to Mildred Harris). It is appropriate, therefore, that Charlie does not fall instantly in love with Merna, as he had with Georgia Hale in *The Gold Rush.* Rather, he rebukes her for stealing his meager rations, only showing her tenderness when she reveals that she is a fellow sufferer, a victim of her father's abuse. Merna lacks Georgia's guile, her sole fault being a weakness for tightrope-walkers. She justifiably betrays her circus-owner father by letting Charlie know that he is not just a propertyman but "the hit of the show." Although she provides Chaplin with the saddest ending of all his silent films, she is entirely without malice. Blissfully, she swings on the trapeze, "looking for rainbows," unaware of the great pain she is inflicting on the Tramp below.

Merna's character becomes the cause of Charlie losing his ability to be funny, and Chaplin could not help but think that Lita Grey was playing the same role in his real life. It was a period of deep depression for him which, combined with major production mishaps, including a disastrous fire, made the filming of *The Circus* his greatest ordeal. As David Robinson has observed, "The most surprising aspect of the film is not that it is as good as it is, but that it was ever completed at all."

The Circus is explicitly about the nature of comedy, and it poses a great paradox in the Tramp's inability to be anything but *inadvertently* funny. Chaplin, the funniest man in the history of the world, after all, achieved his results only through the most conscious and painstaking efforts. The resolution of the paradox lies in the narrow context of the circus itself, where comedy is formalistically purveyed in a theatrical and artificial manner by the traditional clown. Chaplin's genius, however, opens up an entirely separate and transcendent genre— the comedy of character—the comedy inherent in the real world. Certainly Chaplin's comedy had its roots in the traditions of stage funny business, clowndom, and mime (as he personally had training in the English music hall), but the naturalistic qualities and versatility of the motion picture afforded the opportunity to go beyond the strictures of the past. This made possible not only his own enduring legacy but the works of Ernst Lubitsch and René Clair, of Leo McCarey, Preston Sturges, and Frank Capra, and led ultimately (with mixed results) to the "situation comedy" on television.

Chaplin gently mocked the circus clowns with his disruption of their barbershop and William Tell routines, formulized acts which could be funny when well executed (the Tramp himself laughs hysterically as a spectator), but which lacked the extra dimensions of his own great set pieces in *The Circus:* the funhouse, the lion's cage, and the nightmare on the tightrope. (Even the tiny, typically inspired throwaway moments, like the Tramp tipping his hat to a chicken which has just laid an egg on demand, convey more truth than the contrived artifice of the clown routines.) These extra dimensions come clearly from what we know of Charlie's character and personality as conveyed to us by Chaplin's extraordinary acting and by his incarnation of our friend, the Tramp, for fifteen years. Chaplin implicitly rejects being compartmentalized as a clown in favor of being considered a fully rounded person, who happens to be funny. Thus, the Tramp is only funny in the circus ring by accident, explicitly *not* being funny when he is trying to be a clown. It is worth noting, of course, that in the interim since 1928, the cinema and its poor cousin, television, have all but wiped out circuses and vaudeville, and clowns border on extinction. So, Chaplin was acknowledging his awareness that he had almost single-handedly wrought a great change in probably the oldest and most valued means of human communication— the capacity to make one's fellows laugh.

It is tragically ironic that, simultaneously, *The Circus* is mourning Chaplin's failure at what seemed for most people the easiest game of life, finding a mate. Robert Florey (later a Chaplin assistant and then a director in his own right) movingly wrote of a chance encounter with Chaplin at the time: "I cannot express what melancholy overwhelmed me in recognizing the total solitude of the most popular man in the world." Chaplin's artful declaration of this solitude in *The Circus* was to become an existential landmark in the history of the cinema.

The first shot of the film has Merna Kennedy, on horseback, ride through and tear a paper star mounted on a hoop. After some initial paternalism toward the young girl (Chaplin was now approaching forty), Charlie gradually falls in love. When he overhears a fortune-teller predict that Merna will

marry someone dark and handsome, a look in the mirror excites him into gleeful frenzy, a lunatic ballet. Yet, when Merna runs away from the circus and finds the Tramp at a moonlit campfire, he makes the supreme romantic gesture of engineering her hasty marriage to the tightrope-walker, personally providing a ring and showering them with rice at the wedding. Two years later, in Josef von Sternberg's *Morocco*, Adolphe Menjou was to similarly sacrifice himself to facilitate the reunion of Marlene Dietrich and Gary Cooper, explaining to embarrassed friends, "You see, I love her. I'd do anything to make her happy." Chaplin, his bitterness and despair concealed from Merna, is publicly recognizing the failure of his private attempts at

union and conceding his apparent inability to provide the surrogate Merna with what will "make her happy."

The devastating ending of *The Circus* finds the Tramp sitting on a box in the center of what had been the ring. The wagons carrying Merna and her new husband have pulled out, leaving him entirely alone. Charlie picks up the tattered paper star through which Merna had ridden, crumples this symbolic remnant of his hopes and fame, and kicks it backward. Then, the solitary figure, the movies' most famous silhouette, inimitably walks away from the camera into a dawn-lit, desolate landscape. It is the most forlornly hopeless image in all Chaplin; indeed, in all cinema.

CITY LIGHTS
1931

City Lights is Charles Chaplin's most perfectly achieved and balanced work. It would certainly be on any short-list of films with which I would care to be stranded on a desert island. By 1931 the silent cinema was effectively dead, although from an artistic standpoint, the same could almost be said, with a few creative exceptions, for sound films. Chaplin's subtitle, *A Comedy Romance in Pantomime*, seems needlessly explanatory and, by implication, apologetic for what was to be and remains the best American film of its decade.

It took considerable courage to lavish two years of rather expensive production on a silent film to be released in 1931 (and even more courage with *Modern Times*, five years later), but Chaplin felt he had very little choice. He correctly perceived that the Tramp would lose his poetry and grace, if he were coerced into the leveling mundaneness of human speech. He foresaw that sound would force him to sacrifice the "pace and tempo" he had so laboriously perfected. To a degree, this proved true with regard to the Tramp-variant barber in *The Great Dictator*. But in that 1940 film, Chaplin's first talkie, he compensates by playing a second role, a brilliant caricature of Adolf Hitler, which cried out for sound.

Chaplin, like most intellectuals of the period,

saw no advance in the replacement of silent films by those that talked and, even more commonly at the time, squawked. A few directors (Sternberg, Lubitsch, Clair, Hawks, Vidor) had done admirable work in creatively distilling the better qualities of both sound and picture. Ninety-nine percent of what was released while *City Lights* was in production, however, was ghastly and far below the standards of 1928, the last year silent films predominated in the American cinema.

City Lights, with its synchronized track, uses sound for Chaplin's own purposes, poking fun at the talkies and establishing moods through a musical score composed by the director. For the always essential purpose of conveying feelings, asserting the primacy of the heart, Chaplin was adamantly eloquent in his wordlessness. As *Monsieur Verdoux* and *Limelight* were later to prove, he was not at a loss for words, but he believed words, themselves, were a loss. They were intrinsically cheaper and less emotionally exalting than what Jean Cocteau called "the language of the heart"—the language of mime. Eventually, the realities of commerce and then age caused him to make five sound films without the Tramp, but he held out against "progress" for more than a decade and made perhaps his two greatest films sailing against the wind.

The despairing Tramp of *The Circus* has found comfort in the opening of *City Lights,* sleeping like a baby in the lap of a woman. Unfortunately, she is made of stone, one of three figures symbolizing "Peace and Prosperity." For Charlie, as usual, there is neither, and his sojourn in the lap is interrupted by the unveiling of the statue before an assembled throng. Unintentionally offending the multitude (getting a sword up his pants, sitting on the face of one of the male stone figures, and then stepping on its crotch), Charlie escapes to encounter another female statue, this one nude, transforming him instantly into an art connoisseur. Only then does he encounter the flesh-and-blood woman around whom the romance of *City Lights* is constructed, the blind flower girl played by Virginia Cherrill. The Tramp's polite tenderness, posing as a gentleman of means, and the purity of their courtship are intercut with Charlie's efforts to cope with the folly and frenzy of city life, the urbane juxtaposed with the urban.

The embodiment of the city's menace and temptation, Charlie's nemesis and his "friend for life," is an alcoholic millionaire played by Harry Myers. *City Lights* marks the beginning of a significant effort on Chaplin's part at social criticism, which was ultimately to cause him grief in reactionary postwar America. Although obliquely, Chaplin does begin to suggest that the Tramp's problems stem, not from acquiescent poverty or lack of initiative, but from something having to do with the class struggle.

Chaplin and Harry Myers

Shortly after the film's release, Chaplin told an interviewer: "Unemployment is the vital question, not Prohibition. . . . If there is to be any hope for the future it seems to me that there must be some radical change." Millionaire Myers is obtuse and irresponsible, his intermittent generosity and humanity breaking through only when he is drunk. He does not deserve his wealth, especially if the blind girl can't pay her rent and noble Charlie is reduced to cleaning up elephant droppings and having his brains battered in the boxing ring to make a few bucks. The Tramp has always sought fairness in his personal dealings with minimal success, but the clear implication of *City Lights* (and the theme which becomes central to *Modern Times*) is that

Chaplin now aspires to a universal justice for all the "little fellows." With the onset of the Depression, statues proclaiming prosperity deserved to have their faces sat upon, and Charles Chaplin had decided he was just the little fellow to do it.

The City, which had been the Tramp's home and shelter in most previous films, now took on a more hostile and sinister character. Young newsboys harass him in the streets. Traffic swirls around him, and holes open up in the sidewalk. Everywhere he encounters the Mephistophelian Myers, who tempts him with wine, women, and song and then invariably rejects him when he sobers up. The millionaire's world is one of nightclubs and parties, and the intoxicated Tramp is singularly incapable of

Chaplin and Virginia Cherrill

coping with the general mayhem or with the fickleness of friendship. Myers is prone to suicide, but his ineptitude endangers Charlie more than himself; after being shot at and nearly drowning, the Tramp winds up spending nine peaceful months in jail.

Although the Tramp never changed, inevitably Chaplin did. He was now in his forties, and his hair had turned white in the course of his legal disputes with Lita Grey. He also perceived that the world was turning uglier around him. The threat to his career posed by sound films and the fact that he felt lonelier than ever can only have added to his perplexity. Somehow, in spite of or because of this, *City Lights* brought forth from him a lyrical romanticism far more intense than in his earlier work. Like all romanticism, it was dependent on a denial of the present, a retreat from reality.

The American cinema had already developed a tradition in this vein, from Griffith's *True Heart Susie* and *A Romance of Happy Valley* through Frank

Borzage's *Seventh Heaven* and *Street Angel*, whose titles alone speak volumes (or more appropriately, reels). The apogee had been reached in 1927 with a film by the German émigré F.W. Murnau, *Sunrise*. Chaplin seems to have been aware of these works. His carefully prepared sets bear resemblance to those of the Borzage and Murnau films. Griffith's idyllic ruralism and Murnau's depiction of the wholesome countryside as an antidote for urban decadence also find echoes in *City Lights*. When trying to dissuade the drunken millionaire from suicide, Charlie's first impulse is to tell him, "Tomorrow the birds will sing." Virginia Cherrill's occupation, purveyor of flowers, marks her as a pastoral and redeeming intruder in the city, for flowers, like pets, are reassuring reminders of what we city-dwellers have given up in creating our artificial environment. Chaplin frequently returned to the redemptive quality of nature and the open road, a concept reaching its fullest expression in a

rustic fantasy sequence in *Modern Times.* In *City Lights,* the flower girl and her flowers represent all that is clean and pure; she is the real thing—a true monument to peace, prosperity, and uncorrupted humanity.

In both their first and last scenes together, the girl gives Charlie a flower, and their hands touch, the most chaste yet highly charged form of human contact. Hers is an apparitional beauty to him, innocent to the point of being untouchable. In her presence, the Tramp is made more innocent, too, his anxieties and combativeness soothed by her otherworldliness. Significantly, they meet only in daylight, a time less dangerous and unpredictable than the city of night, a time more conducive to the

poetic dream they share. Even when Charlie takes advantage of the girl's blindness to peer at her through her window, there is no prurient violation of her platonic trust, merely a reinforcement of romantic illusion. Lest Charlie become too immersed in his reverie, Chaplin changes the mood by having him knock over a barrel of water, nearly drowning a neighbor, and later subjecting the Tramp to a blow on the head from a flowerpot, unceremoniously dislodged by a cat.

The girl's blindness provides *City Lights* with some of its funniest moments, all having the effect of reminding the Tramp of the precariousness of the romantic ideal in the modern world, but also illustrating his chivalric and stoic gallantry. When

they first meet, the Tramp slips back to watch the girl while she gets fresh water from a fountain, only to have her unwittingly throw the water in his face. He brings her a bag of groceries and has her feel each item, but he is confounded by the protocol of which end of a duck is appropriate for her touch. He holds a skein of wool for her to ball, but she mistakenly grabs a loose thread from his long johns, and he writhes in noble discomfort while she painstakingly and painfully unravels his underwear. The Tramp for once is devoid of malice because, unlike previous Chaplin heroines, Virginia has set a higher standard by her unreserved adoration of Charlie. Ironically, of course, he must destroy the illusion on which the relationship is based by restoring her sight and revealing himself as the Tramp he really is. It is a risk he must take, made monumental by his experiences with the unreliable women of earlier films and previous marriages and by the fickleness of Harry Myers, standing in for friends whom Chaplin felt had betrayed him.

Chaplin could not have been unmindful of the fact that among the consequences of blindness was the inability to experience that which had become the center of his life, the medium through which he felt most fully alive—the motion picture. By providing the girl with the capacity to see, he was metaphorically giving her the most precious of personal gifts, himself. Perhaps he sensed it was safer to relate through the platonic and vicarious substance of celluloid, however unstable and combustible in its chemistry, still more dependable than the unreliable passions of the flesh.

So the risk is taken, and the girl can now see that her chevalier is a bum, made even more disreputable by his stay in prison. Their reunion is profoundly austere and awesomely moving in its ambivalence. We will never know if the girl can see beyond her sight and beyond Charlie's wrinkled smile, timidly hidden behind a rose. What I think we do know is that the final scene of *City Lights* is, in James Agee's words, "the highest moment in the movies."

MODERN TIMES
1936

If *City Lights* represents Chaplin at his romantic zenith, *Modern Times* most admirably displays his prescient satirical gifts. The relationship he began in the early 1930s with Paulette Goddard, culminating in a secret marriage in China, began to relieve his obsessive loneliness and self-absorption. This, together with extensive travels to Europe and Asia, caused him to turn outward and consider problems beyond the personal. America and the world were in the midst of the Great Depression, and he felt a need to speak out on-screen and off. To some, an actor's involvement in politics and economics seemed highly pretentious, in a pre-Reagan era. David Robinson has cogently pointed out, however, "No one before or since had ever had such a burden of idolatry thrust upon him. It was not he or his critics, but the crowd that mobbed him everywhere . . . that cast him in the role of symbol of all the little men in the world." These throngs sensed that Chaplin, the man who made them laugh and cry, was one of their own, and Chaplin willingly accepted a leading part in (as the subtitle to *Modern Times* says) "humanity crusading in the pursuit of happiness."

The subject of man's increasing subservience to the machine was not new to film. Fritz Lang's silent *Metropolis* (1927) and René Clair's *À Nous la Liberté*

(1931) were both skillful and prophetic, but they lacked the special focus that only the universally beloved Charlie could bring to mankind's plight. The appellation Tramp was, of course, misleading, for Charlie had had dozens of jobs in the two decades since 1914, although his primary skill of pluck made him something less than a careerist. Being a nut-tightener on an assembly line fell somewhere in between the grandiosity of circus star and the grossness of street cleaner. Typically, Charlie does not resent the dehumanizing work itself, but rather the little indignities imposed on his person. The boss spies on him in the toilet, and there is no time to scratch an itch. Once again, Chaplin risks crudeness with a reminder that we are all bodies and not just souls. Appropriately, even the most fundamental of physical functions, eating, is threatened when he is used as a guinea pig to demonstrate a feeding machine.

In one of the most inspired comic sequences ever put on film, Charlie is reduced to a helpless cipher by this merciless figment of industrial imagination, symbolically raped by a manic corncob and a mechanical mouth-wiper in a fit of fastidious frenzy. Food, the most elemental human need, the procurement of which had brought man out of the caves and the trees, had now become perverted by prog-

Paulette Goddard and Chaplin

ress. It is unsurprising that the nut-tightener's nut becomes loose, and the Tramp soon runs balletically amok, wreaking havoc on the factory and his fellow wage-slaves.

For Chaplin, a hallmark of modernity (to be considered more explicitly in *Monsieur Verdoux*) is the contemporary role-reversal of normality and insanity, society's passive acceptance of values that by all previous standards were considered barbaric.

He lays a strong claim to prophecy in suggesting man's ultimate self-destruction in his obeisance to his tools. Although Chaplin was much later to focus on the madness of nuclear war, even by 1931 he was astute enough to proclaim: "Machinery should benefit mankind. It should not spell tragedy and throw it out of work."

Already Chaplin was conscious of being Red-baited for such views, and it is thus with delicious irony that he had the Tramp innocently pick up a red flag just as a labor protest rounds the corner behind him. Throughout *Modern Times*, Charlie is in and out of the asylum and the jail house, society's doss houses for denial of its failings. Eventually, the Tramp solicits arrest as shelter from a world gone berserk. Only his accidental collision with Paulette Goddard's gamine, "the only two live spirits in a world of automatons . . . two joyous spirits living by their wits," allows him to proclaim at the end of the film: "Buck up—never say die. We'll get along!"

Goddard's is an extraordinarily vibrant presence, far distant from the passive and pedestaled heroines of earlier Chaplin movies. Like Charlie, the gamine is a victim of contemporaneity, orphaned by industrial violence and a fugitive from the state's stewardship. She escapes with Charlie's help from the do-gooders, as Jackie Coogan had done, and their companionship more closely resembles that of *The Kid* than any of the more overtly romantic or potentially sexual liaisons in intervening films. As Chaplin said, they were "playmates." Their shared fantasy of future domestic bliss, a house in the country where a cow on command passes the kitchen and squirts milk in the pitcher, is childlike, and delight comes in unrestricted access to a toy department. Chaplin seems to go beyond a critique of industrialization to question more fundamental values, such as socially defined adulthood and the family itself. The self-righteous guardians of conventional morality were correct in assessing Chaplin as subversively anarchic and a threat to their cyclopean vision of the world.

Chaplin must have sensed the contradiction between his passionate need for orderliness and control in his professional and personal lives and his innate rejection of all authority. The Tramp was in a perpetual state of compromise in *Modern Times*, foiling his compatriots' jailbreak, going back to

work in the hated factory, and finally breaking his sacred vow of silence to become a singing waiter. In his dual role in *The Great Dictator*, the solution became a split personality, portraying both the oppressor and the oppressed. With *Monsieur Verdoux*, he was to acknowledge his duplicity and incorporate it into a single character, a mild-mannered mass murderer. Of course, Chaplin was too shrewd to believe he was unique in this duality, knowing, to his horror that each of us can be either child or tyrant in a given circumstance. He remained sufficiently hopeful and arguably naive enough, however, at least through the last speech in *The Great Dictator*, to believe "kindness and gentleness" could ensure that "the way of life can be free and beautiful."

Modern Times has been criticized for its loose construction, but it compensates for this by its persistent inventiveness. Chaplin was quite aware that he now stood alone as a maker of silent films. Regardless of its success or failure, this was almost assuredly going to be the Tramp's last hurrah and Chaplin's farewell to the form. The complexity and ingenuity of the comic set pieces reflect an obvious desire to go out in style. In scenes like the roller-skating department-store inspection and that in which Keystone-buddy Chester Conklin is gobbled up by the machines, Chaplin is insisting one last time on the superior fluency of the visual over the verbal. Words could do nothing to enhance the grace of his movement; nor could they be more articulate than his facial expressions as he dutifully attempts to provide lunch to Chester's disembodied head, precariously protruding from the mechanism. This latter, the latest of Chaplin's classic nurturing scenes, culminates in using a chicken as a funnel through which coffee is poured, the rear end in Conklin's mouth insisting on being one final taste of lovable tastelessness. The Tramp's wits have been

pitted against those of the feeding machine, and Charlie emerges at least its equal in efficiency and Keystone-style cruelty.

Along the way, *Modern Times* pays homage to earlier, less sophisticated Chaplin slapstick, the era of *The Rink*, *The Floorwalker*, and a host of offensive cabaret waiters. There is a sense of Chaplin calling forth the shades of slapstick antiquity, akin to his teaming with Buster Keaton in *Limelight*, in a memorial to that which was being buried, his dearly beloved, the medium of silent film.

Sound (other than music) in *Modern Times* comes essentially from machines: the factory boss on the two-way television, the recorded sales message for

the feeding machine, the radio with its gastritis commercial. It thus becomes identified with the dehumanization process, denaturing life as, he believed, it did the cinema. Finally, the dire straits of poverty force the Tramp to succumb to the role of singing waiter, and Chaplin's voice is heard for the first time. His "performance" bears resemblance to the David and Goliath sermon in *The Pilgrim* and the dance of the rolls in *The Gold Rush*. His animation causes him to lose the words written on his cuffs, which go flying off into the far reaches of the cabaret. The Tramp is left to sing in gibberish, a final defiant comment on the lack of saliency of language. For, in spite of his incoherence, or

Chester Conklin and Chaplin

because of it, Charlie the singing waiter is a great hit. The audience responds to the elegance of his movement, the effulgence of his face, the sublimity of his mime.

Charlie and Paulette run from the machines and the city and escape to the open road. We last see them walking toward the distant mountains, symbolic of the struggling little people of the world. On the soundtrack is the wistful, Chaplin-composed "Smile" ("Smile, though your heart is aching. . . . You'll find that life is still worthwhile, if you'll just smile"). Chaplin's life must have seemed to him more worthwhile than ever, even at the moment he was unmistakably aware that the *métier* which had sustained him for a quarter-century was now irrevocably an artifact of the past. In his maturity, now approaching fifty, he faced new challenges —making "talkies" and saving the world.

THE GREAT DICTATOR
1940

The Great Dictator presents unique problems for the historian and critic, trying to reconcile Bosley Crowther's 1940 judgment that it was "perhaps the most significant film ever produced" with its sometimes flawed execution of Chaplin's grand and noble conception. In the preceding commentaries I have argued that by 1940 (with Murnau dead, Carl Dreyer dormant, Griffith retired, Eisenstein and Keaton fettered by outside controls), Chaplin was not only a survivor of the silent period, but had established a strong claim to being the preeminent film artist in the world. Because Chaplin was a universally recognized and generally beloved personality, whose famous moustache had been stolen by an equally well-known but far less beloved comedian-cum-tyrant, his film on Hitler became an event of worldwide consequence.

Hollywood's major studios had made a half dozen anti-Nazi films in the eighteen months preceding the release of *The Great Dictator.* Warner Brothers' *Confessions of a Nazi Spy* seemed very brave when it was released in April 1939, several months prior to the outbreak of war. It explicitly avoids such realities as anti-Semitism, however, and seems, in retrospect, more an offshoot of that studio's popular gangster cycle than a meaningful political statement.

With Frank Borzage's *The Mortal Storm* (June 1940) and Alfred Hitchcock's *Foreign Correspondent* (August 1940), Hollywood did finally offer works of quality and cogency on the subject. Of course, Chaplin's working methods were such that he was an unlikely candidate to be the first across the anti-Nazi finish line. *The Great Dictator* had been planned in 1938, and production began in January 1939, which would certainly make it first in conception and courage if not in release.

To deem the film a work of propaganda or confine it to a genre, as scores of anti-Nazi movies were to emerge during the war, would be demeaning. *The Great Dictator* is the product of an extraordinary synchronicity, an unprecedented convergence of historical and artistic forces. By this happy accident, we find the century's most emblematic popular artist testing his gifts against the man who embodied the greatest threat in recorded time to civilization, to human freedom, and in fact to art. It is not an overstatement to refer to *The Great Dictator,* as David Robinson does, as "an epic incident in the history of mankind."

It would be foolishly presumptuous to believe that any judgment of this film made today, so far removed from the emotions of its emergence, can be

Henry Daniell, Chaplin, and Jack Oakie

truly just. Perhaps Griffith's manic plea for universal brotherhood, *Intolerance,* would most closely rival *The Great Dictator* in its ambition to change the world, but Griffith's masterpiece is too abstract and fuzzy-minded to sustain the comparison. In its confrontation with the cosmos and deeply felt intent to alter it with a mere piece of art, *The Great Dictator* stands alone on its very special pedestal of aspiration.

Chaplin's audacity is even more remarkable for the fact that he was working in an essentially new medium for him, the sound film. His improvisation and experimentation had yielded to a preplanned script, and, as he had anticipated, something was lost in the subservience to dialogue. *The Great Dic-*

tator does not flow as rhythmically as its predecessors. In part, this can be attributed to the need to cut back and forth between the two disparate plots involving Adenoid Hynkel in his palace and the Jewish barber in the ghetto. Even so, too often Chaplin's verbal wit is outdistanced by his imagery, and there is a resultant awkwardness in the pacing. It is not that the film is not funny, but frequently the obligatory dialogue becomes annoyingly superfluous.

Predictably, some of the cleverest sequences are done with no dialogue whatsoever: the synchronized shaving to Brahms, the coins-in-the-pudding scene, and, of course, Hynkel's ballet with the global balloon. One senses Chaplin's greater com-

fort when relying solely on the facility of his face and body. By comparison, scenes with Billy Gilbert as Marshall Herring and Jack Oakie as Benzino Napaloni ring relatively less true and have resonances of Laurel and Hardy and the Marx Brothers, significant but more pedestrian talents. Chaplin can provide funny one-liners (Commander Schultz: "I always thought of you as an Aryan."/Barber: "I'm a vegetarian."), but this reduces his humor from the cosmic to the merely comic. To succumb to the cliché, when dealing with the most visually expressive of performers, a picture is honestly worth a thousand words.

Perhaps an additional problem for a viewer in the 1980s is the inherent absurdity of Hitler, Mus-

solini, and Company. It is hard to believe that a "medieval maniac," as Hynkel acknowledges himself to be, could have been taken seriously by anyone, much less command the adulation of millions willing to commit crimes worse than murder and even die for him. Where does Chaplin's satire end and the dictators' self-parody begin? With Mussolini, who had not stolen Charlie's moustache, Chaplin seems content to reduce him to a fairly stock Italian bozo with a fat wife and a big mouth stuffed full of peanuts. Hitler, on the other hand, whose circumstances of birth were so similar and separated by only four days from his own, understandably holds a primal fascination for him. Both were endowed with unparalleled charisma and force of personality; yet, their paths and purposes could not have been more diverse—the unchallenged apostles of love and hate.

Commercial realities apart, Hynkel is the solitary justification for *The Great Dictator* as a sound film, and sound—radio—was probably the primary factor in Hitler's astonishing sway over Germany. In a sense, then, the dictator had used and was the creature of the technology that Chaplin had so despised and so long resisted. It is a kind of poetic justice that Chaplin was so skillfully able to turn this (to him) unfamiliar weapon against his ranting nemesis.

The Great Dictator bites most ferociously in parodying Hitler's grandiloquent speeches, and, in the end, it is through this form that Chaplin proposes his antidote for the Phooey's evil insanity. The bland English translations of Hynkel's Germanic tirades are a trenchant commentary on the duplicity of language, and in the expressively vicious gibberish of Hynkel's speech, he is at his most articulately frightful. As he confesses to speechwriter Garbitsch (Henry Daniell), while discussing getting rid of the brunettes after the disposal of the Jews, "You'll make me afraid of myself." Chaplin calls attention to the fact that Hitler as speechmaker is nothing more than another actor, one whose excessive animation and gestures are reminiscent of the lesser talents of the silent screen. It is the era of sound, however, and subtlety has given way to noise, civility to barbarity. Like the Tramp-surrogate barber, awakening after twenty years of amnesia to a very changed and diminished world, Chaplin, after trying to ignore reality, now resolves he must confront it.

Despite the new circumstances, *The Great Dictator* is cut very much from the same cloth as earlier Chaplin. The opening scenes could easily be mistaken for *Shoulder Arms*. Billy Gilbert is standing in

for Mack Swain, and there are lots of touches from the Mack Sennett custard-pie school of comedy. The unreliable Big Bertha and Herring's fascination with zany new devices recall *Modern Times* and Chaplin's concept of the machine as menace. Osterlich (Austria) conforms to his now-familiar green and pastoral paradisiacal alternative to urban horrors, represented here by the storm troopers. The upside-down airplane sequence has a Keatonesque flavor, however, and the participation of Karl Struss, who had helped photograph *Sunrise*, gives the film a degree of camera movement that is atypical.

Paulette Goddard's Hannah (apparently named for Chaplin's mother) is essentially the dirty-faced *Modern Times* gamine now of the ghetto. In her simple wisdom, she is a vital life-force who urges the men on to resistance, swinging a mean frying pan. Chaplin's presentation of the ghetto reflects a naive innocence, its sunlit courtyard recalling the blind girl's home in *City Lights*. The Nazis are too inefficient and stupid for their brutality to be truly menacing, at least until Hannah is beaten, just before the barber's climactic speech. Surely, no one's imagination, save Hitler's own, could have anticipated the ultimate horrors of the concentration camps, and it is doubtful that Chaplin could have so brilliantly captured the zaniness inherent in Naziness, if he could have foreseen the enormity of evil around the bend in the road. When the barber and two other ghetto residents try simultaneously to hide from the storm troopers in a small trunk, it is a Marxian moment out of *A Night at the Opera*. We know now that in reality the men would have been candidates for *Night and Fog*, Alain Resnais's grisly postwar documentary on the extermination techniques at Auschwitz. The easy laughs of 1940 cannot now escape the shadow of the crematoria.

So, in his innocence, Chaplin was able to picture Hitler and Mussolini trying to upstage each other at

the buffet table. The fact that they were depicted gobbling up sandwiches and strawberries instead of the final vestiges of civilization reflects Chaplin's failure to appreciate the full implications of the importance of destroying them, but it does not diminish the poignancy of his courageous efforts to try.

In the greatest of cinematic ironies, the Tramp-like barber is mistaken for the dictator and forced into making a speech to announce the annexation of Osterlich. It is a moment made infinitely more ironic by the fact that Chaplin, the man whose mistrust of words had become legendary, steps out of character and delivers a daring personal appeal to a despairing humanity. Schultz tells him, "You must speak. . . . It's our only hope," and who is to say that Chaplin did not believe that this speech, and *The Great Dictator* itself, were not humanity's only hope? And who is to say that this appeal wrenched from the "little fellow"'s gut, giving mankind a timely kick in the collective butt, did not save the world?

MONSIEUR VERDOUX
1947

The world was such that it would not stay saved for long. With the revelations of the Holocaust and the A-bomb, Chaplin's hopeful vision of "the glorious future" turned bleak. Although the 1940s provided him with his greatest personal joy in his marriage to the young and devoted Oona O'Neill, it was also the period of his most bitter frustration and disappointment. In reviewing *The Great Dictator,* Bosley Crowther had spoken of the "faith and surpassing love for mankind which are in the heart of Charlie Chaplin." In the seven years since, Chaplin inevitably had undergone a change of heart. The fraudulent Joan Barry paternity suit and virulent reactionary attacks for his early and dedicated efforts to come to the aid of the Soviets, then America's allies, fed off each other and turned Chaplin into a pariah for many in an ill-informed public. The combination of his private anger and public sense of responsibility produced his darkest and most complex film, *Monsieur Verdoux: A Comedy of Murders.*

Chaplin had come a long way—from the days of sliding on banana peels to going to the guillotine spouting heartfelt aphorisms and foreboding prophecies—and for many who had adored the Tramp, this evolution was unfathomable. For Chaplin, now approaching old age as a serious and self-conscious

artist, it seemed perfectly natural to want to impart his wisdom to the world, whether the world wanted it or not. The resulting film is as stark and black as the Vietnam Veterans Memorial it might ultimately have made unnecessary if *Monsieur Verdoux* had been seen and heeded by his massive old audience of idolators. Instead, at least in his adopted country, the film was vilified unseen, and its painful truths ignored by all but a few perceptive critics. Chaplin had moved left as America moved right, and he now confronted pint-sized Hynkels on all sides. *Monsieur Verdoux* provided his enemies with the perfect instrument for their lunatic crusade against him.

Chaplin was neither anti-religious nor pro-communist. His films contain many allusions to the Bible, including the final speech in *The Great Dictator,* and he was far too self-centered and independent to swallow any political dogma. He was essentially a freethinking democrat and humanitarian. Before Cold War politics had demoralized Western intellectuals into making the unthinkable not only thinkable but mandatory, there was a brief postwar interlude in which rational people could project a different future for the world—one not based on an endlessly futile arms race and a nuclear deterrent built on pillars of barbarism. Chaplin, alone among major Hollywood artists, swiftly

entered into this breach with a work of devastatingly Swiftian irony. Henri Verdoux saw that the logical extension of capitalism was murder and foresaw that technology would shortly provide the means to make these business "killings" on a planetary scale. Although Chaplin understood that Verdoux's fate must be the guillotine, he seemed genuinely surprised that the response to his film bearing Verdoux's philosophy would be vitriolic. To a degree, this confused hurt became the motivation for his next two projects, *Limelight* (1952) and *A King in New York* (1957).

Aside from his parody of Hilter, Verdoux was the first screen persona he had realized for himself since the Tramp. Although he is French, Verdoux's closest physical resemblance is to the late Douglas Fairbanks, particularly in the film's final scenes. Fairbanks, who had served as something of an older brother to the comedian, was a sometime *chevalier* on-screen (*The Three Musketeers, The Iron Mask*), and probably this Gallic gallantry entered into Chaplin's conception of the character. The recurrent motif of flowers (Verdoux picks roses as he barbecues one of his wives in the backyard oven; he frequently visits a florist like the one in *City Lights* to send bouquets to a prospective victim) brings back memories of the Tramp (who, also like Verdoux, was not lacking a larcenous streak). Like Hynkel, Verdoux makes brief, spontaneous attacks on the piano. It must also have crossed Chaplin's mind that he could exploit his own occasional misogynistic and wife-murdering fantasies, and the sartorially immaculate Verdoux must have been a great deal like the older Chaplin in real life. So it is evident that Verdoux's richness as a character sprang from several sources beyond Orson Welles's calling Chaplin's attention to the original French Bluebeard. Of course, it is the actor's superbly nuanced performance that elevates the characterization from the clever to the classical.

Like Sternberg's *Morocco*, Hitchcock's *Vertigo*, and Dreyer's *Gertrud*, *Monsieur Verdoux* is one of the great cinematic explorations of romantic obsession. Verdoux sacrifices all—his honor, his sanity, and finally his life—in an attempt to shelter his invalid wife and his child from a world that has gone out of control. Even though he is capable of concern for a caterpillar and repeated charity toward cats, his relations with all humans except his family are utterly duplicitous. The young woman on whom he intends to test the poison (Marilyn Nash) becomes another exception, when he learns that she, too, had cared for an invalid spouse and shares his manic romanticism: "I'd have killed for him." Verdoux decides against poisoning her, saving it for the policeman who has uncovered his cadaverous career, thus symbolically avenging himself on all the cops who had harassed the Tramp since 1914.

The several exchanges of philosophy with Nash throughout the film grow out of the last speech in *The Great Dictator* and lead to even longer dialogues with Claire Bloom in *Limelight*. Although Verdoux says "words are so futile," Charles Chaplin, the archetypal artist of the silent screen, had found a growing need to verbalize his thoughts and feelings. It could be argued that he had over-adapted to sound and over-reacted to the frightening new experience of being out of touch with his audience. At the same time, Chaplin's speeches are so sincere and soulful, one is inclined toward indulgence.

Surely, from a cinema public that has lionized the agonizingly tortuous gut-spewing of Ingmar Bergman, Chaplin's superior artistry entitles him to a measure of patience and respect. *Monsieur Verdoux* is, after all, a quite fearless personal testament and polemic, essentially a new phenomenon in film history, and it is important to Chaplin to be precisely understood. The points he is making here do not lend themselves so easily to his old and more universally accessible tools of gesture and facial expression, as did pure pathos, comedy, and the infinite ambiguities that lie between them. *Monsieur Verdoux*, like the guillotine, has something inescapably finite about it, as when the hero decides he'd like his first taste of rum before he gives himself to the executioner, while politely rejecting the more abstract ministrations of a priest, a purveyor of guilt and forgiveness but nothing to warm the gullet.

Monsieur Verdoux was made much more quickly and efficiently than *The Great Dictator*, and it shows greater comfort with the techniques of sound. The clever device of having Verdoux narrate the film from his grave was to be used three years later in another masterly exercise in cynicism, Billy Wilder's *Sunset Boulevard*. Chaplin's film is largely lacking in the usual belly laughs, and when they come, they are predictably visual: Verdoux's furious speed at counting money, his expression and balletic panic when he thinks he's been poisoned, the maid's horror at losing her hair. Most of the humor relies on a very dark mordancy, akin to the tone of Hitchcock's later *The Trouble with Harry* and *Psycho*. Martha Raye, as the most durable of Verdoux's wives, has Paulette Goddard's vitality enhanced to a level of frenzied ferocity, a tastelessly dressed orgasmic nightmare with the destructive energy of a whole regiment of storm troopers. Although the classic rowboat scene, with its echoes of Harry Myers's attempts to drown himself in *City Lights*,

Martha Raye and Chaplin

would undoubtedly have been funnier without dialogue, Raye's supremely irritating voice generally enhances her horror. Her obscenely loud laugh in the wedding-party sequence is nearly as chilling as Hynkel's diatribes against the Jews. In this long sequence, Chaplin returns to his roots, relying on physical comedy to good effect.

Music is used very effectively to convey emotions, and one detects the first bars of the "Smile" theme from *Modern Times*, used to introduce the invalid wife and her son. The theme is used again for Marilyn Nash, after Verdoux has decided that he shares a bond of ruthless romanticism with her. It thus becomes a kind of Chaplin signature and a signifier that those characters belong to a dead past, a world safe for Tramps and other innocents.

Verdoux is the Tramp grown old and forced by the responsibility of family to participate finally in the games of life. He plays with poetic *élan* and creative intelligence, but he, like all the other players, must pay the price: little slivers of his soul. We see him age, as we have seen Chaplin age. The spontaneous sweetness of the Tramp is in Verdoux a forced performance, a faucet turned on or off to meet the needs of survival. Only after he has lost his family, his responsibilities, can he be free to give in to the forces of society and allow himself to be arrested, like the Tramp of old. This time, however, there is no release in the next reel. Society has become too strong, and he has become too old. The century's premier rebel has outlasted his time, and the only solace left is the soothing peace of the guillotine.

LIMELIGHT
1952

If *Modern Times* had been a poignantly graceful valediction to the silent cinema, *The Great Dictator* "an epic incident in the history of mankind," and *Monsieur Verdoux* a unique polemic prophesying the imminent end of that history, then *Limelight*, too, has its own very special niche in the annals of film. It is the first in a short line of works that have come to be known as "old men's films," a very specialized and limited genre composed of the subjective summations of the masters of the medium, the pioneers of the cinema.

Not all of the great filmmakers lived to a qualifying age, a too-early death robbing us of late works from Murnau and Eisenstein, Lubitsch and Max Ophüls, Jean Vigo and François Truffaut. Others lost the opportunity to make personal statements in their old age through commercial failure or other mischance. These would include Griffith, Sternberg, Welles, Keaton, and Abel Gance. A handful of the great cineastes did provide us, however, with at least one film of distilled purity from their mature years, expressing their deepest feelings and commenting with considerable intimacy on their lives, careers, and values. Among the most notable of these films are Ford's *The Man Who Shot Liberty Valance* (1962), Dreyer's *Gertrud* (1964), Hawks's *El Dorado* (1967), and Visconti's *Death in Venice* (1971).

All of these works share certain characteristics; they are melancholic, nostalgic, and contemplative; they are austere in emotion, if not always in style; they are the assured work of mature artists; and they run the risk of being too personal, too intimate, too close to the bone. As lovers of the cinema, we should feel privileged to have these men confide in us, offering up their memories, confessions, and vulnerabilities—their realization and acceptance that, as the subtitle of *Limelight* suggests, "age must pass as youth enters."

Thus, *Limelight* in its own trailblazing way reflects as much of Charles Chaplin's courage as had been exhibited by his defiance of "talkies," his challenge to Hitler, and his speaking out against the insanity of the Cold War–driven arms race. Perhaps it took even more bravery to examine in such a public way the open wounds of his pain and insecurity. Chaplin had now come full cycle from *The Circus*. The private hurt of 1928 had been replaced with a fulfilling family life and an apparently ideal marriage. The public adulation for his comedy, however, had given way to venomous disdain for his politics and seeming lack of patriotism. The most striking images from *Limelight* are the haunted close-ups of the elderly Calvero (Chaplin), peering through the camera's lens into an empty theater, seeking his lost

audience. It is as though the public has mimicked the Tramp at the end of *The Circus,* turning away and leaving him as he had left it, in mournful solitude.

Limelight, like *The Circus,* is an artfully tormented exercise in self-therapy, seized upon by Chaplin's critics as self-pity, even solipsism. To reach this latter appraisal is to ignore the fact that Chaplin's whole *oeuvre* was an uninterrupted flow of self-expression, personal testament, and autobiography. He, unlike any other filmmaker, had allowed his soul to stand naked before us. In this, Chaplin is close to the openness and candor of modern literature, which has interwoven our lives with those of Whitman and Joyce, Hemingway and Proust.

The Man Who Shot Liberty Valance is an exploration of the craft of cinematic storytelling and legend-making, a statement of disappointment with modernity, and a grimly pensive confrontation with the inevitability of death. *Limelight* similarly considers the nature and art of comedy and the distasteful fate that awaits us all. Both are magnificently moving and frequently profound films, but because Chaplin appears on-screen as his own protagonist, he runs far more risks than John Ford, who can lurk in the giant shadow of John Wayne. Chaplin's Calvero may be too sentimental and self-pitying for some, but the compensation is substantial—perhaps the most intensely felt performance in the history of the

cinema. *Limelight* is Chaplin devoid of frills and facades, and, as such, it is quintessentially beautiful and true—the late Matisse of the movies.

The personal quality of *Limelight* is accentuated by Chaplin having made it a family affair. His half brother, Wheeler Dryden, plays the neighborhood physician, and five of his children appear in the film, including his second son, Sydney, as his rival for Claire Bloom's affections. Even Oona Chaplin appears as a double for Bloom in some long-shot retakes. The prewar London that Chaplin depicts is the London of his youthful career as a stage and music-hall performer, the youth he had left behind permanently by 1914 to join Mack Sennett in the California sunshine. It is a London of sweet memo-

ries, peopled with street musicians, aggressive theater-lounge tarts, and palmy tearooms—a simple, hopeful time lost forever in the Great War.

It seems disconcerting to consider that *Limelight,* a film whose fundamental message is hope, begins with a suicide attempt and ends in death. Chaplin is acknowledging a sense that his own end is near (actually, he lived another quarter-century), but that he will live on in his children, in his artistic legacy, and in memory. He was intensely proud of his earlier films and frequently rescreened them for family and friends. Still, he seemed now to distrust their oblique silence and is ever more insistent on imparting his philosophical wisdom. At times, *Limelight* teeters on the brink of becoming an essay or a lecture. This discursive quality is something it shares with the other valedictory films mentioned earlier. Like Ford, Dreyer, and Hawks, Chaplin had made enough films of self-evident artistry that he knew he had gratified us. As in a post-orgasmic moment, he was now determined to talk about the meaning of that gratification, and as our lover for forty years, he is entitled to our attention and indulgence.

Such reflective pauses seem to me not to diminish *Limelight* as a work of Chaplinesque inspiration but rather to enhance its value. As he did at the end of *The Great Dictator* for other urgent reasons, Chaplin steps out of character or, better still, beyond character to offer us a very nearly Brechtian commentary on those (especially himself) strutting and fretting on his celluloid stage. The urgency inherent in envisioning his own death, embattled as he was on all sides, produced the declaration by Calvero: "Truth is all I have left." *Limelight* is the truth as Charles Chaplin saw it. One assumes he generally subscribed to Calvero's dictum that "time . . . always writes the perfect ending," but Chaplin also could see no harm in adding a few pungent aphorisms of his own to help time along.

Actually, *Limelight* is not without virtues in a conventionally cinematic frame of reference. The other performances are essentially the best in any of Chaplin's sound films, and twenty-year-old Claire Bloom as Thereza is wonderful in her adult debut. She has the gentle qualities of Paulette Goddard's gamine, but as the most complex female character Chaplin ever created, the emotional range of her portrayal is a clear sign that the director's relationship with Oona had a calming and enlightening effect on his attitudes toward the other sex. Although there are a few regrettable lapses into inferior back projection, Karl Struss's moving camera prowls fluidly through some fairly lavish sets.

The final scene is particularly "cinematic" as Calvero's death is photographed in long-shot, with Buster Keaton and Sydney Chaplin hovering above him as symbols of past and future. The camera moves in as he is covered with a sheet and then tracks backward as Claire Bloom dances into the frame, perfectly visualizing the theme that "age must pass as youth enters."

Limelight is only intermittently funny. Calvero's flirtatious and scatological charm reflects his Trampy antecedents, but Chaplin does not choose to provide him with the major comic sequences included in all his previous and subsequent films (except, of course, *A Woman of Paris*). The obvious reason is that they would be out of character for a comedian who has lost touch with his muse. Most of the funny business, with emphasis on the latter word, is reserved for Calvero's stage performances as depicted in his dreams and the final gala tribute that is staged for him. While these are amusing and clever, they are constrained by the proscenium; they are *acts*, enacted in the theatrical limelight. They are what Chaplin told us in *The Circus* he had transcended, as the world had become his stage; they are not what he liked to call "realistic"—and were not therefore timeless.

Thus, although Calvero had developed a formidable following as a "tramp comedian," Chaplin makes it clear that Calvero was not *the* Tramp comedian. Calvero's art may have been what Chaplin imagined, in retrospect, would have been his *métier*, if he had not taken the fateful step of taking a chance on the movies. Clearly, Chaplin enjoyed performing Calvero's routines, perhaps most notably the ghostly silent duet with his old rival Buster Keaton, but it seems obvious that he had no illusions that these divertissements approached the comedic inspiration of his films of the 1920s and 1930s. They do show an endearing

Chaplin and Claire Bloom

nostalgia for his youth, for a career that might have been, and, in the Keaton sequence, for the career that was but was no more. As early as *The Kid,* Chaplin had set his sights on something beyond comedy. In *Limelight,* comedy becomes merely a conveniently comfortable tool for use in his larger enterprises of soul-searching and summing-up.

Chaplin in *Limelight* is curiously candid in his self-mockery. Calvero makes jokes about having had many wives, calls himself "an old sinner," and is referred to by Nigel Bruce as "that old reprobate." He is totally nonpolitical, and the bitterness so evident in *Monsieur Verdoux* shows through only in a single speech calling the public "a monster without a head." Calvero seems genuinely to embody Chaplin's newfound "feeling of sad dignity . . . fatal for a comic." Calvero's phrase prophesying the circumstances for Bloom's future liaison with Sydney Chaplin—"the elegant melancholy of twilight" —seems to best describe his state of mind as he

made the film. Chaplin actually allows himself to cry on-screen for the first time, and Bloom extolls "his sweetness, his sadness." Although events and longevity contrived for him to make two more films, there can be no misconstruing Chaplin's intent that *Limelight* should serve as his final testament on matters of personal import, on the accrued wisdom of his mind, on the vital concerns of his heart.

Although *Limelight,* like Chaplin's life, is scattered with disappointments, the ultimate thrust is toward romance and a zest for life: desiring to see Terry dance one more time; wanting to continue, though stuck in a drum. If *Limelight,* like the tribute to Calvero, is not "the greatest event in theatrical history," it is, at least, a uniquely self-revelatory and touchingly brave event in cinematic history. As his father-in-law, Eugene O'Neill, had made peace with his family demons in *Long Day's Journey into Night,* so Charles Chaplin made moving and haunted art of his own accumulated spirits in *Limelight.*

TWO LATE FILMS:
A KING IN NEW YORK, 1957
A COUNTESS FROM HONG KONG, 1967

It would be singularly ungrateful to arbitrarily dismiss Chaplin's two final films as inferior to his other work. Although such a judgment is essentially valid, both of these movies offer enough pleasure on their own terms and are so imbued with their creator's personality as to warrant our patient consideration. To measure them against Chaplin's best, after all, is to hold them to the highest of standards, a pinnacle to which very few motion pictures can aspire. Chaplin had lavished his deepest passions on the preceding films, and *A King* and *A Countess* show perhaps less a declining talent than a relaxed urge to entertain and amuse, an honorable purpose reminiscent of the artist's younger days.

While *A King in New York* seems a bit scattered in its energies, it is not lacking in satirical intent. In many ways, it appears designed to confirm Chaplin's prophecies in *Modern Times* on the dangerous directions in which technology was leading. The link between the two films is made specific by the fact that the opening shots of the revolutionary mob storming the king's palace are almost identical to those of the workers at the beginning of *Modern Times*. Television once again intrudes on the privacy of the bathroom, now with the added irritation of commercials.

Unsurprisingly, Chaplin is distressed by the continuing annoyance of bombastic sound, his nemesis of long-standing. In the streets, in the theater, in a supper club, the noise of New York relentlessly pursues the king. Because of the din in the restaurant, he can place his order with the waiter only through his gift for mime.

For the first time, Chaplin's own medium becomes a target for his satiric thrusts. He decries sex, violence, and the recent innovation of the wide screen, which he cleverly compares with sitting at the net in a tennis match. On the whole, Chaplin is more bemused than bitter at the way the world has turned, comfortably ensconced as he now was on the laurels of his Swiss mountaintop. He takes easy swipes at the crassness of the American nouveaux riches and elaborately takes to task the vulgarity of American commercialism. In the old days, bad breath or body odor might have been fit subjects for slapstick humor, but now, to Chaplin's chagrin, they are brought up at fancy dinner parties.

Reluctantly, the king decides to cash in on his advertising potential, capitalizing on his "majestic stuff" and "lots of dignity," as his account executive puts it. When he decides to pursue his new career as a liquor spokesman (ominously anticipating Orson Welles's later bent in peddling cheap wine),

Chaplin pokes gentle fun at his elderly appearance by being persuaded to have a face-lift. Appropriately, it becomes undone while laughing at a nightclub slapstick routine borrowed from his 1915 Essanay film *Work*. America's maniacal preoccupation with youth, captured early in the film by Chaplin's depiction of the hysteria of the new rock-and-roll fad, is just a bit too silly for a man now approaching seventy to take very seriously. And for those put off by the spectacle of his lechery toward Dawn Addams, bear in mind that he was still siring children four years after *A King in New York* was released.

As always, there are echoes of earlier work. The film affords us the opportunity of seeing Chaplin perform a snippet from *Hamlet*, with his soliloquy resembling nothing so much as one of Adenoid Hynkel's flailing speeches. The pea-shooting progressive school boys bring back memories of similar scenes in *City Lights*, and there are lots of evocative, glittering little moments of slapstick with Chaplinesque musical accompaniment. *A King in New York* only really becomes fully focused, however, when Chaplin takes up the subject of the contemporary American political crisis, known in retrospect as McCarthyism.

After the completion of *Limelight*, Chaplin (still a British citizen) took his family on a holiday abroad, only to discover while on the high seas that, to its everlasting shame, the Truman Administration had announced he would not be permitted reentry without establishing his moral worth. In part, this came at the urging of Senator (soon to be Vice President) Richard M. Nixon. The decade-long reactionary campaign against Chaplin now crested, and as with earlier messiahs, the authorities chose to make an example of him. *A King in New York* was both a personal response to this outrage and cinema's only contemporary statement on the hysteria that still raged in the United States five years after Chaplin's departure.

Confronting the HUAC/McCarthy axis seemed similar to taking on Hitler and Mussolini, in that it was hard to satirize targets that were so inherently absurd that they themselves bordered on self-parody. In *The Great Dictator*, it was the innocent barber who was victimized in order to dramatize the depravity of Nazism. In *A King in New York*, Chaplin makes the sympathetic innocent a ten-year-old boy played by his own son Michael. The king becomes a secondary victim through his association with young Ruppert, and the king, in an obvious reference to Chaplin's problems resulting from *Monsieur Verdoux*, says, "I lost my throne because I didn't want atomic bombs." Most of Chaplin's anarchically libertarian philosophy, however, is put in Ruppert's mouth, and it is (ironically) understood

that he is spouting what he has been told by his parents. When the king questions Ruppert on what provoked his political confrontation with a visiting atomic-energy committee, the boy trenchantly comments on Chaplin's own inability to avoid controversy: "I just get started, and I can't stop." The sad-eyed Ruppert has become Chaplin's alter ego in much the same way Jackie Coogan had been thirty-six years earlier.

The fear inspired by being summoned to testify before HUAC, causing physical panic in the king and his obviously Jewish lawyer, closely parallels the fear of the ghetto residents when Hynkel makes his most inflammatory anti-Jewish radio speech. Since the Rosenberg trial, of course, strong undercurrents of anti-Semitism had surfaced in the anticommunist crusade, and Ruppert's family name, Maccabee, had Old Testament resonances of its own.

Finally, after years of being hounded and harassed, Chaplin's response to an incipient American fascism is (as my friend Bo Smith has observed) the same as his response to the full-blown German variety, the best response possible for the world's greatest comedian—being funny. He returns to his gift for low comedy, for slapstick, getting his finger stuck in a fire hose (in effect, giving HUAC the finger) and then turning the hose on the self-styled guardians of right thinking and moral worthiness (showing us that they are literally all wet). Chaplin is saying that his basic intent all along has only been to make us laugh—questioning the right of these upstarts to turn the government of the world's most important democracy into a low farce, trying in the process to steal his *métier* as Hitler had stolen his moustache.

Early in the film, the king had undergone the indignities of immigration procedures, replete with fingerprinting and the rude barrage of journalists.

Chaplin was both recalling the Joan Barry trial and anticipating what it would be like to attempt reentry into the United States. At the end of the film, the king concludes that it's "too crazy here. . . . I'll sit it out in Europe." Chaplin was eventually to return to America with dignity, in glory and triumph, in 1972, having the last laugh on the soon to be disgraced Richard M. Nixon by coming back during the year of Watergate.

Chaplin's 1936 trip to the Far East with Paulette Goddard (during which they were secretly married) had inspired an unrealized project called *Stowaway*. In his Swiss retirement, Chaplin reworked this script into a shipboard romance called *A Countess from Hong Kong*. What might possibly have been a silent vehicle for Paulette and himself became a film starring Sophia Loren and Marlon Brando using not only sound but color and

Sophia Loren

CinemaScope. The passage of thirty years had taken its toll on both the concept and the director, resulting in a work of occasional charm and amusement, but a film nonetheless flawed and disappointing.

Marlon Brando, arguably the greatest movie actor to have appeared since Chaplin himself, is terribly miscast. Devoid of a genuine comic spirit or romantic instinct, Brando was aggressively resistant to Chaplin's direction. Rather than imitate Chap-

lin's acted-out performance of his part, which was always the director's basic methodology, one suspects the rebellious actor was parodying Chaplin's own officious and, in Brando's eyes, demeaning manner. In any event, the long and awkward bedroom-farce sequences, which would have had a dubious chance of success with even Cary Grant in the part, are rendered tedious by Brando's gracelessness and uninterest.

Chaplin directing Geraldine Chaplin and Marlon Brando

Chaplin puts in a brief appearance, credited as "an old steward," warning of rough seas with the line: "Just a little sloppy, nothing serious." This is sadly and ironically descriptive of much of the film, which suffers not only from poor continuity but also major gaps and incongruities in the narrative. Such things are more or less forgivable in a film that is working, but *A Countess from Hong Kong*, with its only mildly diverting repartee and fitful inspiration, cannot expect such indulgence.

Certainly, a greater on-screen presence by the project's "steward" would have helped, and one is particularly regretful that Chaplin didn't find a way to perform together with the delightfully doddering Margaret Rutherford, whose tiny, two-minute scene

as Miss Gaulswallow is the funniest in the film. Even more so than was true with *A Woman of Paris*, one must conclude that a genuinely Chaplinesque film must have Charlie himself as its heart and soul.

It is only fair to say that, of all filmmakers, Chaplin, through his vast and prolonged success, had earned the right to fail. Studio directors like Ford, Hitchcock, and Hawks made many mediocre films interspersed with their great ones, and *A Countess* might have been better if Chaplin (and his co-workers) was not so convinced, based on his past record, that he could do no wrong.

In fairness also, *A Countess* does not lack minor virtues. While Chaplin is not exactly innovative in his use of color (the pigments of his imagination tended toward the pastel) or wide-screen, the film generally has an appealing visual quality in those scenes (about half the running time) not confined to Marlon Brando's stateroom. Patrick Cargill's fay butler, forced into a phony marriage with Sophia Loren, momentarily reincarnates Henri Verdoux when he naughtily tells her, "Whatever your desire is, I'm always at your service." Miss Loren herself was not unsympathetic to and responded well to Chaplin's direction. In comic scenes, she is capable of becoming almost Tramp-like, and her moments of close-up sadness virtually replicate haunting memories of Calvero. The spirit of *A Countess* is unmistakably Chaplinesque. As Andrew Sarris has said, "It is the quintessence of everything Chaplin has ever felt . . . in his frayed lace-valentine heart."

Chaplin manages to slip in a few polemical potshots, such as comparing politics to murder, arson, rape, and show business. The countess's state of statelessness must have had special meaning for him, and when Brando says he is saddened by her "aloneness," it cannot help but make us think of our old friend, the Tramp.

The ending, with Brando spontaneously giving up all for Loren, is the most deliriously romantic since *The Gold Rush*, appropriately so for Chaplin, who through several trials and many errors had finally found personal happiness, two decades before. Brando asks, "May I have this dance?" The couple glides gracefully together about a cabaret floor that is lined with palms, and Chaplin's lush, sentimental strings on the soundtrack transport us back a half-century, to when it all began for him on other palm-decorated cabaret sets on little movie stages in California. The dead past has become present and alive again in that private and immortal universe bequeathed to his public by Charles Spencer Chaplin.

AFTERWORD

It seems self-evident that any appraisal of Charles Chaplin is doomed to inadequacy by the very quintessence of his genius. While one can write in extensive detail on the editing techniques of Griffith or Eisenstein or the camera movements of Murnau and Ophüls, Chaplin's acting, as he was painfully aware, transcends the capacity of language. We can analyze the brilliant cyclone sequence in Keaton's *Steamboat Bill, Jr.* to the point where we can begin to grasp how it works, but no amount of analysis, I think, can unveil the mysteries at the heart of the final moments of *City Lights.* Andrew Sarris was correct in asserting that Chaplin's face is his *mise en scène.* No amount of words, however artfully arranged, can capture the nuances of Chaplin's expression in innumerable close-ups, living flesh exuding feelings simultaneously fleeting and eternal. Nothing can be said, no matter the care taken and detail given, to truly describe the poise and grace of a perfect and precise movement or gesture that emanates not so much from Chaplin's conscious design as from the secret processes of his soul.

Chaplin, himself, was fittingly fond of the word ineffable. It was his destiny to exemplify ineffability in performance, and he must take the blame for this writer's and others' dilemma. If one looks at the films of other comedic actors—great (Keaton), near-great (Harold Lloyd, Harry Langdon, Laurel and Hardy, the Marxes, Peter Sellers, Woody Allen), and mediocre (Abbott and Costello, Martin and Lewis, the Three Stooges)—one sometimes finds things borrowed from Chaplin, and one also finds that he sometimes borrowed from his peers. Yet, the same basic gags and situations become in Chaplin's hands (in his body, in his face) somehow more felt, more sincere, more human. To misquote Gertrude Stein, there's more there, there.

René Clair writes that Chaplin was so "profoundly original" that he had little direct influence on the cinema, but that without Chaplin, "*we* would not have been altogether the same people we are today." The great Jean Renoir said: "The master of masters, the film-maker of film-makers, for me is still Charlie Chaplin.... One may say...that he has made only one film and that every facet of that film is a different enactment of the same profession of faith.... [Clifford Odets] telephoned that he wanted us to meet the Chaplins. It was like inviting a devout Christian to meet God in person."

Because Chaplin's effect on us has been so pervasively godlike, it becomes hard to reconcile his Olympian status with what we know of this all too fragile and imperfect little man, laboring away in a tiny corner of that vulgar twentieth-century phenomenon we think of as the movie business, rubbing elbows with mere mortals of dubious morals and even more dubious talents. Somehow, Charles Chaplin rose above this, on-screen if not off, and created a body of work that can reassure us, in moments of doubt, that human beings are worth something more than our daily newspapers or daily lives would have us otherwise believe.

If, as Alexander Woollcott said, the Tramp is "the finest gentleman of our time," then Chaplin has done us the supreme service of providing the ultimate role model. For such emulation, we need not wear a derby or carry a cane, but we should look within ourselves for that little bit of Charlie we all have, that capacity to love, to persevere, to laugh at our pretensions.

The silent movies, because of their accessibility to all and their far greater emotional potential than television's small screen, were the perfect medium for Chaplin's purposes. Had he been born a generation later, he might have become a successful actor, even actor/director, but his opportunities for total independence, experimentation, and the honing of his skills would not have existed. His career would probably have resembled the frustrated and fragmented one experienced by Orson Welles, trying to convince the pygmies of power that he was a giant. So it was extraordinary luck (both his and ours) that made it possible for Chaplin to parlay his dedication and natural gift into a celluloid legacy.

What will the future think of that legacy of our "finest gentleman"? Will they laugh, and will they cry? Can Chaplin transcend the boundaries of time as he did those of language, place, and nationality? I can only hope that the human spirit never becomes so impoverished that it will not long for love, for laughter, or even for the opportunity to kick some annoying clod in the butt. I suspect that sometime in another century, a colonist will be sitting on Mars, his or her face lit by the reflected flickering of an image of a strange little man in antique clothing waddling down a dusty road on a distant planet; and I suspect our descendant will laugh and share Harold Clurman's belief that Charles Chaplin was and is "a man to be cherished."

Chaplin in *The Pilgrim*

FILMOGRAPHY

1914

All films listed for 1914 are Keystone Film Company productions, produced by Mack Sennett and directed by Charles Chaplin, except as indicated.

Making a Living. Dir: Henry Lehrman

Kid Auto Races at Venice. Dir: Henry Lehrman

Mabel's Strange Predicament. Dir: Henry Lehrman, Mack Sennett

Between Showers. Dir: Henry Lehrman

A Film Johnnie. Dir: George Nichols

Tango Tangles. Dir: Mack Sennett

His Favorite Pastime. Dir: George Nichols

Cruel, Cruel Love. Dir: George Nichols

The Star Boarder. Dir: George Nichols

Mabel at the Wheel. Dir: Mabel Normand, Mack Sennett

Twenty Minutes of Love

Caught in a Cabaret. Dir: Mabel Normand

Caught in the Rain

A Busy Day

The Fatal Mallet. Dir: Mack Sennett

Her Friend the Bandit. Dir: unknown

The Knockout. Dir: Charles Avery

Mabel's Busy Day. Dir: Mabel Normand(?)

Mabel's Married Life

Laughing Gas

The Property Man

The Face on the Bar Room Floor

Recreation

The Masquerader

His New Profession

The Rounders

The New Janitor

Those Love Pangs

Dough and Dynamite

Gentlemen of Nerve

His Musical Career

His Trysting Place

Tillie's Punctured Romance. Dir: Mack Sennett

Getting Acquainted

His Prehistoric Past

1915–16

All films listed for 1915–16 are Essanay Film Manufacturing Company productions, produced by Jesse T. Robbins and directed by Charles Chaplin.

His New Job

A Night Out

The Champion

In the Park

A Jitney Elopement

The Tramp

By the Sea

Work

A Woman

The Bank

Shanghaied

A Night in the Show

Charlie Chaplin's Burlesque on Carmen

Police

1916–17

All films listed for 1916–17 are Mutual Films, produced and directed by Charles Chaplin.

The Floorwalker

The Fireman

The Vagabond

One A.M.

The Count

The Pawnshop

Behind the Screen

The Rink

Easy Street

The Cure

The Immigrant

The Adventurer

1918–23

All films listed for 1918–23 are First National Films, produced, directed, and written by Charles Chaplin.

How to Make Movies. 1917 or 1918. (A comedy-documentary of new Chaplin studios; never released)

A Dog's Life. 1918. Edna Purviance, Mut, Sydney Chaplin

The Bond. 1918. Edna Purviance, Sydney Chaplin, Henry Bergman

Chaplin-Lauder Charity Film. 1918. Harry Lauder. (Never completed; unedited)

Shoulder Arms. 1918. Edna Purviance, Sydney Chaplin, Jack Wilson

Sunnyside. 1919. Edna Purviance, Tom Wilson, Tom Terriss

A Day's Pleasure. 1919. Edna Purviance, Marion Feducha, Jackie Coogan

The Professor. 1919. (Never completed)

The Kid. 1921. Edna Purviance, Jackie Coogan, Carl Miller

Nice and Friendly. 1921(?). Lord Louis Mountbatten, Lady Edwina Mountbatten, Jackie Coogan. (Never released)

The Idle Class. 1921. Edna Purviance, Mack Swain, Henry Bergman

Pay Day. 1922. Phyllis Allen, Mack Swain, Edna Purviance

The Pilgrim. 1923. Edna Purviance, Mack Swain, Charles Reisner

1923–52

All films listed for 1923–52 are The United Artists films, produced, directed, and written by Charles Chaplin.

A Woman of Paris. 1923. Edna Purviance, Adolphe Menjou, Carl Miller. (Chaplin in cameo role)

The Gold Rush. 1925. Georgia Hale, Mack Swain, Tom Murray

The Circus. 1928. Merna Kennedy, Allan Garcia, Henry Crocker

City Lights. 1931. Virginia Cherrill, Harry Myers, Hank Mann

Modern Times. 1936. Paulette Goddard, Henry Bergman, Chester Conklin

The Great Dictator. 1940. Paulette Goddard, Jack Oakie, Henry Daniell, Billy Gilbert

Monsieur Verdoux. 1947. Martha Raye, Isabel Elsom, Marilyn Nash, Robert Lewis

Limelight. 1952. Claire Bloom, Buster Keaton, Sydney Chaplin, Nigel Bruce

1953–77

The films listed for 1953–77 are British Productions, produced, directed, and written by Charles Chaplin.

A King in New York. 1957. Maxine Audley, Oliver Johnston, Michael Chaplin, Dawn Addams

A Countess from Hong Kong. 1967. Marlon Brando, Sophia Loren, Sydney Chaplin, Tippi Hedren. (Chaplin in cameo role)

Produced by Chaplin

A Woman of the Sea. (Working title: *Sea Gulls*). 1926. Charles Chaplin Film Corp. Dir, sc: Josef von Sternberg. Edna Purviance. (Never released; on June 24, 1933, the negative was formally burnt.)

Compilation Film

The Chaplin Revue. 1959. Roy Film Establishment–United Artists. Pro, dir, sc: Charles Chaplin. (*Shoulder Arms, A Dog's Life, The Pilgrim*)

The Unknown Chaplin. 1983. Thames Television. Dir: David Gill and Kevin Brownlow. Three-part documentary featuring outtakes and rehearsal footage as well as the unreleased *How to Make Movies* and the uncompleted *The Professor.*

Other Film Appearances

His Regeneration. 1915. Essanay Film Manufacturing Company. Dir: Broncho Billy Anderson. With Anderson; Chaplin as himself

The Nut. 1921. Douglas Fairbanks–United Artists. Dir: Theodore Reed. With Douglas Fairbanks; Chaplin as himself

Souls for Sale. 1923. Rupert Hughes–Metro Goldwyn Mayer. Dir: Rupert Hughes. Chaplin appears as himself along with many other Hollywood stars

Show People. 1928. Cosmopolitan–Metro Goldwyn Mayer. Dir: King Vidor. With Marion Davies; Chaplin as himself

The Gentleman Tramp. 1975. Filmverhuurkantoor "De Dam" B.V.–Audjeff. Dir: Richard Patterson. Compilation documentary, with newly filmed scenes of Chaplin at home in Corsier-sur-Vevey, Switzerland

APPENDICES

**Appendix I:
The Second Coming**

[In 1972 Charles Chaplin was invited back to the United States to be fêted by Lincoln Center in New York City and to receive a special Oscar in Hollywood. I wrote the following piece, reprinted from *Film Comment* (September 1972), on the occasion of the former event, Chaplin's first visit to New York since his exile began, twenty years before.—C.S.]

When his mother came to this country . . . they had her over on Ellis Island. When she went over there, they started to question her. And they said, "Are you the mother of Charles Chaplin?" And she said, "I'm the mother of Jesus Christ" . . . *she was "shell-shock," supposed to be.*

—Rollie Totheroh

I knew Chaplin was coming back to America before there was a public announcement. As the word got out, and as I subsequently discussed the visit with my friends in the film world, I am afraid I astounded a great many people by saying, in effect, that this would be the preeminent event of our lifetime. For my adult interest and ultimately my career in films had begun with the 1964 Chaplin retrospective at the Plaza Theatre in New York. Never

before or since have I been so shaken by an artist and his art, and it is unlikely that I will ever quite recover my bearings. In weak moments, I have even fancied changing my middle name from the rather pedestrian Alan to Chaplin, thus becoming his namesake in full recognition of my status as his soulsake.

This piece will be nothing if not a delirious and shameless love song for the man whom I consider the most worshipful religio-mythological being who has ever lived and, incidentally, the best damn maker of movies, too. Feeling this way, therefore, I found more than a touch of poetic irony in the anecdote told by Charlie's longtime cameraman about Charlie's mother (*Film Culture*, Spring 1972). And it doesn't matter much to me if some people consider me " 'shell-shock,' supposed to be."

Time is the great author. It always writes the perfect ending.

—Calvero in *Limelight*

How would the most devout Christian in New York cope with a visit by Jesus to the Plaza Hotel? How was I to cope with the comparable situation, especially living right around the corner as I do? In 1964 I was a crewcut virgin from New Jersey. By 1972 I had become a scraggly, jaded New Yorker—closer now to Monsieur Verdoux than to the Little Fellow. Eight years ago I might have gone to the hotel in all innocence as an autograph-seeking toady. Now, even though this no longer seemed properly dignified, the temptation was too great. I swallowed my sophistication and went the first night.

Charlie had stayed at the Plaza in 1916, when he was waiting to sign his contract with Mutual for all the money in the world. Now after fifty-six years of the most incredible career any human has experienced, he came back. Sitting beside the elegant Palm Court that Monday evening, amidst violins and Victorian ambience, I could understand why he had chosen this hotel. Surely if any of the gracefulness of life in 1916 survives in New York, it breathes most freely in the lobby of the Plaza. After a period of wandering about the Palm Court indulging myself in this luxury, I proceeded to eavesdrop at the front desk, query men's-room attendants, and ride elevators, finally ascertaining that Charlie had rooms on the twelfth floor.

Anxious and slightly inebriated, I arrived there and discovered the corridor deserted except for two men walking ahead of me. It was immediately obvious that these were detectives assigned to protect my hero from the likes of me. (This is not to say that I have a special knack for spotting plainclothesmen. The fact that one of them had a pair of handcuffs dangling ominously from his back pocket rather gave them away.) Since they knew where in the huge rectangle of rooms Charlie's suite was, however, and I didn't, I decided to follow them.

By this point, I felt about as comfortable as the little barber impersonating Adenoid Hynkel and preparing to address the crowd during the *Anschluss* of Osterlich. I had never been upstairs in the Plaza before, and I was impressed as I proceeded on my perilous pursuit by the enormous width of the hallways. I thought irreverently that this must be the reason Orson Welles is fond of the place, having the space here to comfortably navigate the great bulk he acquired by failing to heed Marlene Dietrich's advice, in *Touch of Evil*, to "lay off those candy bars, honey."

After we had gone most of the way around the rectangle, the cops became aware of my presence and stopped to question me as to why I was there. I told the truth, and so did they: Charlie and his entourage were at a dinner party (Gloria Vanderbilt Cooper's) and would

not be back till late. Somewhat relieved, I went home, happy in the knowledge that I had retained enough foolish romanticism to have made the effort. I knew that I would see Charlie the next evening at Philharmonic Hall, and that it would be curiously easier to make a public display of my love for him than to have done it in private.

Terry: I still love you.
Calvero: Of course you do. . . . You always will.

It is not my purpose here to make a critical case for Chaplin's surpassing genius. If anything definitive on that subject can be said in a few brief pages, James Agee and André Bazin have already done it most eloquently. And although I respect the efforts of the authors whose articles appear elsewhere in this issue of *Film Comment*, more than likely the case for Chaplin cannot be adequately made in a roomful of written words. Andrew Sarris has pointed out that Chaplin's face is his *mise en scène*, and Chaplin's face is as ineffable as (Gide says) is happiness. Charlie's consummate genius derives from his ability to reflect his soul in his eyes—an expression of transcendent, divine, perfect humanity, more sublime and artful than all the magic and montage at the command of other filmmakers.

To remove the emotional element from the consideration of a film's worth is to deny to the cinema its most important gift and its *raison d'être*. For those unfeeling hearts and castrated spirits who can look at the great masterworks from *The Gold Rush* through *Limelight* and not be overwhelmed, I can only express sorrow. They are invariably those for whom the essence of cinema is either a detached and pensive study of a structurally complex cold meatball, or else the instant eyestrain of fragmented views of Colorado landscapes and vaginal areas photographed through lenses smeared with Brylcreem by cameras mounted on kangaroos. And they are committed to a "modern" aesthetic, the ultimate goal of which is a cinema of computer printouts on celluloid—cold, irrelevant, antihuman—devoid of all those little idiosyncrasies that civilized man has cultivated and cherished for centuries; devoid of the individual personality. Their art is worse than dead. It is boring! There are no one's agonies and joys visible between the frames. Chaplin, in his most mature and self-aware films, gives us the most intently felt and eloquent testament of what it is to be a human being. I believe this to be the loftiest purpose and the highest pinnacle of achievement of all artistic expression.

It has become a cliché to fault Chaplin for his lack of bravura technique. As Rollie Totheroh said, "He just didn't have much patience with the technical side of it." Although one can legitimately argue that the actual viewing of films like *The Great Dictator* reveals an astonishing fluidity, in the final analysis Chaplin never felt the need to compete with the brilliant hocus-pocus of Murnau, Eisenstein, and their gifted protégé, Welles. Chaplin's style was profound in its simplicity, and he was always too preoccupied with depth of feeling to worry about depth of focus.

As much as I respond to the stylistic virtuosity of Sternberg and Ophüls, surely Chaplin's peers in the realm of romanticism, their films lack the warmth of their master's. The hearts of Adolphe Menjou (*Morocco*) and Danielle Darrieux (*Madame de...*) may break, but we never quite feel our own has cracked in two as we do at the end of *The Circus*. Griffith and Hitchcock are intermittently brilliant (usually when they are at their most manic and perverse), but their work, like Chaplin's own *A Woman of Paris,* is frequently too closely bound to the limiting conventions of melodrama.

Ford and Renoir, my two favorites after Chaplin, have been too erratic in their long careers—they've made too many bad films to reign supreme. Their romantic vision and humanistic orientation seem slightly less pure, contaminated by their association with the studio system and its compromises. Chaplin's financial independence did, indeed, give him an advantage, but he gained it through his success. Ultimately, we must base our judgments on what exists on celluloid, and when all the *oeuvres* have been run through the projector, I believe one cannot escape the conclusion that Chaplin has no equal.

The difference between Keaton and Chaplin is the difference . . . between man as machine and man as angel. . . .
                                        —Andrew Sarris

In recent years, thanks to the fortuitous reappearance of his classic films, Buster Keaton's reputation has been reestablished, at Chaplin's expense. Even Sarris has lent his prestige to this campaign by harping on Chaplin's "solipsism," this despite acknowledging that every Chaplin film from *A Woman of Paris* through *Limelight* was the best American film of its year. Sarris recently passed up all of Charlie's works to select Buster's *Sherlock, Jr.* as one of the ten best films of all time. *Sherlock, Jr.* is, indeed, superbly clever in its stunts and gimmicks, and it raises a multitude of questions regarding the respective realms of illusion and reality in the cinema. It remains, however, superficial and cold, a film of blatantly obvious virtues easy for critics to cite—a film, as Sarris has said of others, "for anthologies."

As a body, Keaton's films lend themselves far more easily to critical analysis than Chaplin's. Everything is visible on the surface and simple to describe. There is a vigor and glory in Keaton's films, but they lack the profundity, development, and wholeness of great art. More often than not they reflect the fact that Buster was still a young, unsure artist experimenting, learning—not yet mature. Films like *Battling Butler, Seven Chances, The Three Ages,* and *Go West* are only sporadically inspired, having a good sequence here, a dull one there. The other works, especially *The General,* are better; they are as good as anything Chaplin did before *The Gold Rush.*

The tragedy, the terrible pity of Keaton's career can be seen in the collapse evident between the excellent *The Cameraman* and the quite bad *Spite Marriage.* Keaton was destroyed at thirty-three, the age at which Chaplin had made nothing more formidable than *The Kid.* What Keaton might have accomplished had he been permitted to make his own films as a mature artist we will never know, and I mourn for those lost films as much as anyone. To consider him Chaplin's equal on the basis of what actually exists, however, is wistful nonsense.

Then live without hope . . . life for the moment. There are still wonderful moments.

—Calvero

There is something a trifle obscene about Chaplin materializing in the flesh in a hall built for the likes of Leonard Bernstein. Perhaps he should have flown in on angel's wings *à la* the dream sequence of *The Kid,* the film we were to see. Alas, Charlie will probably be among the angels all too soon, even if it is his expressed desire to go to Hell—the climate there being much warmer for an old man than Switzerland. April 4 was not a night for thoughts of mortality, however; it was the night Chaplin was, as he put it, "reborn."

There were those who complained that the buffet was not up to what they expected for their $100. There were those who wanted a long speech and a live performance in Tramp costume. And there were some of us who were ecstatic over the few simple words, the eloquent gestures, and the unique opportunity to look upon that visage which is the quintessence of all that is human. Through the generosity of a wealthy benefactor, I was seated in the orchestra among the gentry just below Charlie's box. And as he looked down, threw kisses, and smiled the tearful smile reserved (one had thought) for Virginia Cherrill, I could not help but feel that the pink face topped with its white mane of antiquity was smiling just for me. And that last kiss blown from the loveliest of male hands—clearly it was aimed in my direction.

. . . human society never accepts him even provisionally except as a result of a misunderstanding.

—André Bazin

I suppose it was, in retrospect, too perfect. A small part of me regrets that Charlie didn't revert to the Tramp's character just for a moment and pee on all those tuxedoed millionaires and on this phony trying to "pass," as the Tramp had done so many times. But Oona would have scolded him, and by 1972 it was too late for such a grand and elegant gesture. Charlie was old

enough now and sentimental enough to want to be loved even on terms his former enemies could accept—this was, therefore, a self-created misunderstanding for the purpose of saying hello again in order to say a gentle and poignant goodbye.

So we are left with his myth and with his films. Both are only as ephemeral as life is on this planet. For, if there is a legacy of the twentieth century for which posterity will not damn us, nothing in it is more durable and beauteous than the fifty miles or so of celluloid that the Little Fellow left behind on his way to Hell.

Appendix II:
A Tribute to Sir Charles Chaplin

[This piece is reprinted from my program notes for April 21, 1978, at The Museum of Modern Art, New York.—C.S.]

Charles Spencer Chaplin was born eighty-nine years ago this week in London. Sir Charles Chaplin died Christmas day last year in Vevey, Switzerland. In between he became the most popular man in the world and one of the greatest geniuses of our time.

The comedies created by Mack Sennett in the early 1910s were among the best and most typical of their era. Sennett had learned basic film technique from D. W. Griffith, but he saw little reason to apply Griffith's subtlety with performances and narrative to his crude slapstick. Sennett's films were enormously popular and, ofttimes, inventive. His cinema was a one-reel filmic Feydeau, his studio a factory without a roof.

One day he hired a little-known British stage comedian whose artistic aspirations at the time went no further than the title of his first film, *Making a Living.* Twenty-four-year-old Charlie tips his hand, however, by stealing a camera in his first few minutes on film. In *Kid Auto Races,* his second film, Charlie's main function is to keep intruding on the frame in an improvised and intoxicated manner in what is ostensibly a documentary on a soapbox derby. This is the first time we see Chaplin's own derby and the rest of his ineffable sartorial splendor.

These early films, which find Chaplin at the mercy of other, noncomprehending directors, are indeed crude, crying out for close-ups and less frantic pacing. Later in 1914, with Charlie himself at the helm, one finds greater complexity of situation, more creative camera placement, and a willingness to forswear the quick gag for the long take. In an ambitious two-reeler like *Dough and Dynamite* we discover the young actor/director experimenting with an essentially new genre, the comedy of character. Political critics of Chaplin might note that this is a "right-wing" film, with the Tramp heroically scabbing against striking Bolshevik bakers.

It would take many years for Chaplin to outgrow the essentially cruel roots of slapstick humor. Some of the most delicious moments of these early films are also the most malicious. In *The Property Man* he sadistically pins an old man under a trunk and then climbs on top and kicks him in the face. In *His Musical Career* he tricks Mack Swain into drinking varnish, and in *His Trysting Place* he wipes his sticky fingers in an old man's beard and pulls out a flea. He is vulgar and rude, but there are glimpses of what is to come when this same film ends with a close shot of an idyllic family portrait.

With his move to Essanay in 1915 Chaplin's comedy immediately becomes less frenetic. The same violent bits of the Keystone period become graceful and balletic, more deliberately artful. By *A Jitney Elopement* (his fifth Essanay film) we see him torn between his emerging need for careful camera placement to capture the nuances of character, in the first reel, and a reversion to a long-shot Keystone-like car chase in the second.

The next film was *The Tramp*, and from here on there was no turning back. His character has been formed, however sketchily. There is no more posing; he is only Charlie. It is a film of violence (in his hands, every object becomes a weapon), vulgarity (he obscenely contemplates milking a bull), and, most significantly, pathos (Charlie having been rejected by Edna Purviance limps down the road, then shrugs, and quickens his step).

An element of tenderness has entered his work, and for the next half-century Chaplin's comedy was never again to be just funny. Even his attempts at tenderness, however, were often tinged with violence. In his very next film (*By the Sea*) he attempts to gain Edna's sympathetic attention by sticking her with a splinter plucked from his behind. In *Limelight*, he restores Claire Bloom's grasp on life by brutally slapping her, and in his most tenderly romantic role, as Monsieur Verdoux, he plays a mass murderer.

Verdoux tells the streetwalker, "This is a ruthless world, and one must be ruthless to cope with it." The dichotomy is raised with her response: "That isn't true. It's a blundering world, and a very sad one . . . yet a little kindness can make it beautiful."

Perhaps the most striking thing one finds in viewing several dozen early Chaplins in a short span of time is the degree of repetition. Plots, situations, gags keep reoccurring, always more polished but often derived from his early, rather primitive films. Some of the very best sequences of his brilliant features had rehearsals decades earlier. The teetering cabin sequence in *The Gold Rush*, for example, is lifted from *Shanghaied*, and *Police* gives us the same flophouse as *The Kid*; the whole of Chaplin's first little masterpiece, *The Vagabond*, is, in fact, a dry run for *The Kid*.

By the time Chaplin signed his Mutual contract in 1916 he had become the richest and most famous entertainer in the history of the world. It is forgivable for him to show a bit of narcissism in *The Floorwalker* when he playfully kisses a Chaplin look-alike. The fact that the other character is a thief may be its own comment on the rash of Chaplin imitators who had sprung up at other film studios.

With the release of *The Vagabond*, Charlie became truly inimitable. It opens with the classic image of his feet approaching the camera from behind the swinging doors of a tavern. He is carrying the violin he was to play thirty-six years later in *Limelight*, and he must compete for an audience with a bunch of besotted street musicians similar to those he accompanies one drunken night in that film. *The Vagabond* is an archetypal little film, the first of the genre one can only define as Chaplinesque. For fifty more years, encompassing nearly thirty more films, a self-consciously mature man named *Charles* Chaplin defined the limits of a personal universe in a manner unparalleled in cinema and, in the opinion of some, unequaled in the annals of human expression. For us, Charlie's audience, we're all a bit like Hetty Kelly, the recipient of his first puppy-love affair, about whom he understatedly said: "That night I went home feeling triumphant, for I had touched her with my sadness and had made my personality felt."

Buster Keaton has been justly praised for his perpetual and ingenious contest with the hazards of the physical universe. Long before Buster started making his own films, however, Chaplin was charting some of the same territory. *One A.M.* is a classic example of objects assuming lives of their own, turning Charlie's living room and bedroom into obstacle courses and making the simplest human functions acts of survival. Two decades later, he was to expand on this theme in the masterly *Modern Times*, decades in which, in Charlie's vision, people had to use all their human resources to avoid being mere adjuncts of machines. It is by his very human vulnerability, the feelings with which Chaplin permits us to identify, that his art becomes more profound than that of Keaton. Although Buster's films lend themselves to intellectualized cosmic abstractions, Charlie exposes his sorrow and his smile, and like the rest of us, he is subject to stepping in dog doody.

Chaplin's Mutual films are each characterized by a particular space or locale from which the logic of the comedy springs. This provides each work with a unity and distinct quality of its own. Chaplin's later features generally are built around one- or two-reel sequences, each with a similar unity unto itself, but tied to the whole by a thin plot and dominated by the most strongly defined and most affecting character the cinema had provided. In essence, virtually his whole *oeuvre* is a continuing autobiography building on the relationship we have developed with Charlie. Because of the candor with which he shares his life with us, there develops a familial intimacy between the Tramp and ourselves. To view a great work like *Limelight* outside of this context is to lose layers of meaning and be unaffected by the reverberations of a lovely man's soul. To criticize Chaplin as too sentimental is to deny our own potential for vulnerability and feeling. To view him as self-indulgent for exposing his own feelings on film is to constrict the cinema to the dimensions of other media, or worse yet, to see movies as mere technical or academic exercises. Simply put, one misses the point.

In *A Dog's Life*, Charlie mistakes a man's crying for laughter. His whole life and career are a commentary on the frail membrane which separates the two. His first great success came at age five, when he replaced his singing mother on the stage after her voice gave out, and his first laugh came in innocently imitating the misery of her cracking vocal chords. (This must surely have contributed an additional trauma to his inevitable decision to give up the security of the miming Tramp and take the risk of having to vocalize the persona of Adenoid Hynkel, in *The Great Dictator.*) Chaplin speculated on the impact upon himself of a childhood incident involving a sheep which escaped on its way to the slaughterhouse. He recalled giggling at the animal's efforts to elude its pursuers and being horrified by the realization that its capture meant its death. "That stark, spring afternoon and that comedy chase stayed with me for days; and I wonder if that episode did not establish the premise of my future films—the combination of the tragic and comic." All his more mature films are haunted by intimations of mortality and the knowledge that none of us has the last laugh. One of the results is a frantic pursuit of some earthly happiness (usually imagined as a pastoral, idyllic romance) paralleled in both his life and his films. That Sir Charles eventually attained his fantasy should lend us all a bit of encouragement in our own frantic scramble down the same road.

In a letter introducing *A Woman of Paris: A Drama of Fate* in 1923 Chaplin emphasized that he was striving for realism, implicitly imputing superficiality to his whimsical comedic impulse. For all its wonderful qualities and its undeniable influence, *A Woman of Paris* still lacks the dimensions of his best work. Aside from Chaplin's own absence before the camera, the vision is too bleak and humorless. In a sense there is a more profound comment on the human condition in Charlie's and Mack Swain's simultaneous slipping on a banana peel in *The Pilgrim* than there is in Carl Miller's lovelorn suicide.

Perhaps Chaplin's own sense of vulnerability made him choose as his fantasy love-objects a blind girl (*City Lights*), a poverty-stricken waif (*Modern Times*), a victimized Jew (*The Great Dictator*), and a cripple (*Monsieur Verdoux* and *Limelight*). In the early films there is seldom any sense that he might actually get the girl, and it is all Charlie can do to survive life's perils himself. Among his major works after *The Gold Rush*, only in *Modern Times* does he permit himself a "happy" ending, as he and Paulette Goddard walk away from the camera together to the bittersweet strains of "Smile." Although the climactic speech at the end of *The Great Dictator* is optimistic, one must presume the soldiers of the double-cross will inevitably discover that it is the little barber disguised as the Phooey and throw him in a concentration camp or worse. In both *Verdoux* and *Limelight* Chaplin dies, but the bitterness of the former's curtain speeches gives way to the dignified sweetness of Calvero's farewell to life. He has transferred his philosophy and vitality to Claire Bloom, who will marry Sydney Chaplin and presumably raise lots of little Chaplins. After all his many struggles, Charlie can now reconcile himself to losing the final one, but with his protégée and progeny carrying on, much as Geraldine and her siblings seem to be doing in real life. As Calvero says, "Time is the great author. It always writes the perfect ending."

I will always remember the night in 1972 at Lincoln Center in the terms used to describe the benefit for Calvero in *Limelight:* "the greatest event in theatrical history." Charlie was now too old and dignified to do a trained flea act, but he was there. Although Chaplin was indubitably British, Swiss by adoption, and as universal as any creature has ever been, it is hard not to think of him as thoroughly American. He lived and worked here for almost his entire career, he shared our values and our sunshine, and it was indescribably moving to have him home again. And it was appropriate that after all the

pain, he returned with his queen holding his frail arm, as a king in New York.

Sir Charles died last Christmas with Lady Chaplin at his bedside. One can imagine him thinking, as Calvero says at the end of *Limelight*, when he falls from the stage into a drum, "I'd like to continue, but I'm stuck." The shock of losing someone many of us believed immortal was followed quickly by the strange abduction of his body with still no clue as to the purpose. One will never again be able to view with a degree of detachment the churchyard ballet sequence in *Limelight* after which Charlie walks by in his clown suit as the grave is wheeled away.

In any event, Charlie's mortal remains, wherever they may be,* must be viewed as of lesser consequence than the miracle that is his celluloid legacy. We can pretty well be assured that for as long as it matters he will be with us, and we need him. René Clair has suggested that if Chaplin never existed the cinema would be much the same; that he was so "profoundly original" as to have little influence on the development of film technique. Clair's point, however, is that had there been no funny little fellow with derby and cane and haunting eyes, "*we* would not have been altogether the same people we are today." As Clair puts it, with perfect simplicity, Charlie is our friend.

---

*[*Chaplin's remains were subsequently recovered.*—C.S.]

Chaplin in *Monsieur Verdoux*